THEOLOGIAN OF RESISTANCE

THEOLOGIAN OF RESISTANCE
THE LIFE AND THOUGHT OF
DIETRICH BONHOEFFER

CHRISTIANE TIETZ

VICTORIA J. BARNETT, *translator*

THEOLOGIAN OF RESISTANCE
The Life and Thought of Dietrich Bonhoeffer

First published in German under the title 'Dietrich Bonhoeffer. Theologe im Widerstand', München: C.H.Beck 2013.

Interior photos used from http://www.dietrich-bonhoeffer.net/downloads/

Cover image: Dietrich Bonhoeffer/Berlin/Art Resource,NY
Cover design: Laurie Ingram

Library of Congress Cataloging-in-Publication Data
Print ISBN: 978-1-5064-0844-6
eBook ISBN: 978-1-5064-0845-3

The paper used in this publication meets the minimum requirements of American National Standard for Information Sciences — Permanence of Paper for Printed Library Materials, ANSI Z329.48-1984.

Manufactured in the U.S.A.

CONTENTS

PREFACE

"Knowledge cannot be separated from the existence in which it was acquired." (DBWE 4:51)[1]

This insight from Dietrich Bonhoeffer goes to the heart of why he has become so well known worldwide. Bonhoeffer's life and thought are so integrally connected that the unusual course of his life makes people curious about his theology, and vice versa: his theological theses are deeply imbued with the experiences of his life. Whoever becomes preoccupied with Bonhoeffer as a person cannot avoid dealing with his theology, and whoever wishes to understand his theology must take note of his life story.

Dietrich Bonhoeffer was one of the leading Protestant theologians in the resistance against National Socialism in Germany, recognizing very early the threats posed by Nazism. He was involved in the founding of the Confessing Church and later became director of one of its preachers' seminaries. During the war years he belonged to the group of political conspirators planning the July 20, 1944, assassination attempt on Adolf Hitler. Imprisoned by the National Socialists, he spent the last two years of his life in prison. Shortly

---

1. Translator's note: here and throughout the volume "DBWE" stands for Dietrich Bonhoeffer Works Edition (the seventeen-volume English translation of his collected writings) followed by the respective volume number and page number.

before the end of the war he was hanged in the Flossenbürg concentration camp.

Bonhoeffer was too radical for some in the Confessing Church, and in the early postwar years his political resistance met with a lack of understanding among many Christians. Later, however, the picture of him became almost universally positive. While there are still voices that dispute the academic quality of his theology, his writings remain widely read today. In church circles he is a welcome source of inspiration, and he is the research focus of countless historians and theologians. The reverence for him has gone so far that Bonhoeffer is sometimes portrayed as an unquestionable hero or a timeless source of wisdom. In the process, a picture of him has emerged that has little to do with the real person and his work.

In contrast, this book is an attempt—with the awareness that over seventy years have passed since his execution—to portray Bonhoeffer in the context of his times, not avoiding the critical questions about his life and work. This is a chronologically written biography that traces the development of his thought. The epilogue sketches the reception of Bonhoeffer and concludes with an inquiry about his contemporary relevance.

CHAPTER ONE

From Breslau to Berlin, 1906–1923

Family Influences

Like many of those Germans who would join the political conspiracy to overthrow the National Socialist regime, Dietrich Bonhoeffer came from a middle-class family. His father, Karl Bonhoeffer, was professor of psychiatry and neurology, first in Breslau (what is today Wroclaw, Poland) and then after 1912 at the Charité Hospital in Berlin. He was the descendant of a middle-class family that had resided in Schwäbisch Hall, a town in the southern part of Germany, since the sixteenth century. Karl Bonhoeffer's mother, Julie Tafel, was a woman whose personality had been shaped by revolutionary and social-ist ideas.

Dietrich Bonhoeffer's mother, Paula von Hase, was the daughter of the pastor and member of the Breslau Church Consistory, Karl Alfred von Hase, who in turn was the son of the renowned Jena professor of church history, Karl August von Hase. Paula von Hase's mother, Countess Clara von Kalckreuth, came from a Prussian artist's family and had taken piano lessons from Clara Schumann and Franz Liszt. As a result, Dietrich Bonhoeffer's family origins were characterized by middle-class ideals, the courage to reform society, a long academic tradition, and the fine arts. All of these different influences can be detected in his life's journey.

Karl Bonhoeffer was a strict and controlling personality. One of his colleagues said of him: "Just as he utterly disliked all that is immoderate, exaggerated, or undisciplined, so too in his own person everything was completely controlled."[1] Academically, he had no use for the psychoanalysis of Sigmund Freud or Carl Gustav Jung, which looked for unconscious or suppressed feelings; this was also true of his son Dietrich, who would always remain skeptical about emotional self-reflection. Karl Bonhoeffer's own approach was based on neuropathology. Although sensitive in his personal dealings with others, he considered mastery of one's own feelings a virtue. He despised idle chatter in himself and in others. The Bonhoeffer children were only allowed to speak at the table when they were asked about the events of their day. Nonetheless, the children cared deeply for their father and always knew where they stood with him.

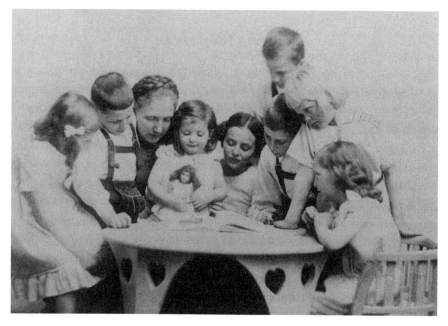

Paula Bonhoeffer with her eight children 1910

---

1. Sabine Leibholz-Bonhoeffer, *The Bonhoeffers: Portrait of a Family* (Chicago: Covenant Publications, 1994), 10.

Dietrich Bonhoeffer's mother was more strongly oriented toward relationships and feelings. "She was full of courage and optimism, and her speech was natural and vivacious. It was a matter of indifference to her what others thought of her; she did what she considered right."[2] Numerous maids assisted with the household. A Moravian woman, Maria Horn, was much loved by the children and helped raise them. Pedagogically trained and having taken the examination to be a teacher, Bonhoeffer's mother instructed the children partly herself and was later assisted by Maria Horn's sister, Käthe. Their mother, however, always was responsible for their religious instruction. She said grace at the table, prayed with the children each evening, and told them Bible stories. It was assumed that all the children would be confirmed in the Christian faith, yet the family almost never attended regular church services.

Dietrich Bonhoeffer and his twin sister, Sabine, were born on February 4, 1906. They were the sixth and seventh children, arriving after three boys, Karl-Friedrich, Walter, and Klaus, and two girls, Ursula and Christine. Susanne, born three years later, rounded out the group. Karl-Friedrich became a physicist, Walter died at the age of eighteen as a soldier in the First World War, and Klaus became a lawyer. Ursula married the lawyer Rüdiger Schleicher and Christine married the lawyer Hans von Dohnanyi. Both men, along with Klaus and Dietrich Bonhoeffer, would be part of the political conspiracy against Adolf Hitler; all paid for it in 1945 with their lives. Sabine married the legal scholar Gerhard Leibholz, and Susanne married a theologian, Walter Dress.

Childhood and Youth in Berlin

The family's move in 1912 from Breslau to Berlin would be decisive for Dietrich Bonhoeffer's life journey. At first the family lived near the center of town, in an apartment close to the zoo. When Dietrich Bonhoeffer was ten years old they moved to a villa in Grunewald, a neighborhood that included renowned figures such as the physicist Max Planck, the church historian Adolf von Harnack, and the historian Hans Delbrück.

Playing music together had a special place in the Bonhoeffers' family life. Dietrich Bonhoeffer studied piano and played regularly until his arrest in 1943. His parents purchased a vacation house, a former forester's cottage, in the Harz mountains in the heart of Germany. Dietrich Bonhoeffer's childhood

---

2. Ibid., 5.

impressions of family vacations there stayed with him to his final prison days. In his prison cell he wrote:

> In imagination I spend a good deal of time outdoors, in the midland mountains in summer, actually, in the forest glades near Friedrichsbrunn or on the slopes where one can look across Treseburg to the Brocken. I lie on my back in the grass, watching the clouds float across the blue sky in the breeze and listening to the sounds of the forest. It's remarkable how our whole outlook is shaped by childhood impressions like these, so that it seems impossible to me and against my nature that we could have had a house in the high mountains or by the sea! It's the central uplands which are my natural environment . . . and which made me who I am.[3]

When they were grown the children recalled a happy childhood, and their family ties remained close, as the numerous letters that passed back and forth between the family members attest. They had a trusting relationship with one another and knew that they could depend on each other, most especially on the support of their parents. Dietrich Bonhoeffer was aware of how good, yet unusual and seductive this was. As a student he once said, "I should like to live an unsheltered life for once. We cannot understand the others [who have not had such a sheltered life]. We always have our parents to help us over every difficulty. However far away we may be from them, this gives us such a blatant security."[4]

The Decision to Study Theology

The schools Bonhoeffer attended were crucial intellectual influences: Friedrichswerder Gymnasium and then the Grunewald Gymnasium (today called the Walther-Rathenau School), which he attended from 1919 to 1923. Both were well-known humanistic secondary schools. These schools met Bonhoeffer's youthful interest in history and literature, philosophy and the arts. Through the boy scouts Bonhoeffer came into contact with the Youth Movement (*Jugendbewegung*) of that era. "Every Sunday morning we do exercises, play war games, and such. It is always very nice," the thirteen-year-old wrote to

---

3. DBWE 8:294.
4. Eberhard Bethge, *Dietrich Bonhoeffer: A Biography*, trans. Eric Mosbacher, et al., rev. and ed. Victoria J. Barnett (Minneapolis: Fortress Press, 2000), 20.

his grandmother.[5] In Berlin, he experienced firsthand political events like the 1918 November Revolution that led to the formation of the Weimar Republic and the 1922 assassination of foreign minister Walther Rathenau; indeed, he was able to hear the fatal shots at Rathenau from his classroom.

The family was surprised when Dietrich Bonhoeffer decided to study theology, since the institutional church played hardly any role in their everyday lives. His father was especially disappointed by the choice of profession. Later, when the Church Struggle reached its most intensive phase, he wrote his son that he had feared "that a quiet, uneventful pastor's life, as I knew it from that of my Swabian uncle and as Eduard Mörike [a Swabian poet] describes it, would really be almost a pity for you. So far as uneventfulness is concerned, I was greatly mistaken."[6] Whatever moved Bonhoeffer to this decision ultimately remains obscure. Perhaps one reason was the early death of his brother Walter in April 1918 on the front, five days after being wounded in France. The entire family was shattered by this loss, and Bonhoeffer's mother had difficulty recovering from it. She suffered for weeks under a strong depression, which was certainly hard for a twelve-year-old boy. For his confirmation Dietrich Bonhoeffer was given his brother's Bible; he kept it for the rest of his life to read and used it as he prepared his sermons.

There were other deaths during the war in the family's circle of acquaintances that troubled the children. Sabine Leibholz-Bonhoeffer later wrote:

> We heard of the death of our older cousins and some of our classmates' fathers. And so in the evenings after prayers and hymn singing . . . we used to lie awake for a long time and try to imagine what it must be like to be dead and to have entered eternal life . . . When Dietrich at the age of twelve got his own room we agreed that he would knock on the wall at night when Susi and I were "to think of God."[7]

The war confronted the children with subjects and questions that normally would have played no role at that age. Later, when he was twenty-six, Bonhoeffer wrote that as a child he liked to think about death and wished for himself an early, God-given death so that others could recognize that "to a believer in

---

5. DBWE 9:30.
6. DBWE 13:97.
7. Leibholz-Bonhoeffer, *The Bonhoeffers*, 32–33, trans. altered.

God, dying was not hard but a glorious thing," while noting at the same time how much he wanted to live—and was ashamed of this internal ambivalence.[8]

Eberhard Bethge, Bonhoeffer's friend and biographer, suspected that in addition to the shock of the death of his brother, "at the root of his choice was a basic drive toward independence" and that ". . . because he was lonely he became a theologian, and because he became a theologian he was lonely."[9] Bonhoeffer himself later recounted that in addition to his personal faith there was a measure of vanity in his decision to study theology, which was spurred by a wish to be the center of attention.[10]

---

8. DBWE 11:397.
9. Bethge, *Dietrich Bonhoeffer*, 37.
10. DBWE 11:394–96.

CHAPTER TWO

THE RETURN FROM TÜBINGEN TO BERLIN, 1923–1927

17yrs - 21

Two Semesters at Tübingen

In spring 1923 Dietrich Bonhoeffer began his studies in Protestant theology in Tübingen, attending the university where his father had studied. He joined his father's student fraternity, "the Hedgehogs," attracted primarily by the conversations and excursions, and didn't ask about its political orientation. He left the Hedgehogs in 1933, however, when the fraternity incorporated the Aryan paragraph, a state law excluding persons of Jewish heritage, into its charter. During his time in Tübingen he also participated in a two-week military exercise, after checking with his parents, for he thought "that the sooner one gets this over with the better; then one can have the secure feeling that one can help in crises."[1]

In Tübingen Bonhoeffer went to lectures by the leading theologians Adolf Schlatter and Karl Heim, but attended with greater interest the courses held by the philosopher Karl Groos, who treated epistemological questions that

the investigation of what distinguishes justified belief from opinion; the theory of knowledge, esp. w/ regard to its methods, validity, and scope

---

1. DBWE 9:70.

7

Dietrich Bonhoeffer as student in Tübingen 1923 (17 yrs)

would intrigue him for several years. Nonetheless, he was not really enthused by Tübingen, and decided after two semesters to return to Berlin.

A Journey to Italy

Before his return, however, he and his brother Klaus took a two-month journey south that would leave him with long-lasting and decisive impressions. In spring 1924 the two traveled first to Rome for two and a half weeks. They were deeply impressed by this city of ancient and Christian monuments, which at the same time was a pulsating modern metropolis. After a Mass held in Trinità dei Monti, a church at the top of the Spanish steps associated at that time with a women's convent, Bonhoeffer wrote in his diary that in the vespers of the novitiates he had experienced "worship in the true sense": "The day had been magnificent. It was the first day on which something of the reality of Catholicism began to dawn on me—nothing romantic, etc.—but I think I'm beginning to understand the concept of 'church.'"[2] Coming from a theology student the comment is surprising. It reveals that for Bonhoeffer at the

---

2. DBWE 9:89.

beginning of his theological existence the real communal life of the faithful as church remained meaningless. This is probably due to the fact that in his own family Christian faith was lived almost completely without reference to the institutional church. It was in Rome that it became clear to Bonhoeffer for the first time—confronted by a church to which people from the entire world belonged—that the visible church and communal worship are essential for Christian life. He was fascinated by the possibility of making confession in the church and receiving the forgiveness of sins. He saw how in the act of confession the believer concretely experiences faith in the community of faith, rather than alone:

> In the afternoon: Maria Maggiore. Important day of confession. All the confessionals are occupied and densely surrounded by people praying. It is gratifying to see so many serious faces; nothing that you can say against Catholicism applies to them. . . . Confession does not necessarily lead to scrupulous narrowness. . . . For those people who are religiously astute, it is the concretization of the idea of the church that is fulfilled in confession and absolution.[3]

The reality of the church in Rome must have made a deep impression on Bonhoeffer. It led him to deal with the question of the role the church plays for faith from the Protestant perspective, both in his dissertation and in his postdoctoral thesis.

After a short trip to Sicily and Tripoli in North Africa the brothers returned to Rome via Naples, and then to Berlin.

Theological Berlin

During that era the professors of the theological faculty at the University of Berlin were the leading scholars in their fields. While the renowned church historian Adolf von Harnack had been emeritus since 1921, he continued to offer seminars for a small circle of students, to which Bonhoeffer was invited. They read texts from the first Christian centuries. Bonhoeffer was impressed by this master of so-called liberal theology, which had been the dominant tendency in Protestant theology for a century. Such theology was critical of the traditional church dogmas and emphasized individual religiosity. Bonhoeffer

---

3. DBWE 9:89.

• leading figure in Neo-orthodoxy movement;
∧ • was deported from Ger. in 1935 after refusing to sign Oath of Loyalty;
• went back to Switz. to teach

was thoroughly skeptical of Harnack's approach, for at the same time he was becoming familiar with the concepts of the great critic of liberal theology, Karl Barth. While defending his dissertation before the theological faculty, however, Bonhoeffer clearly stated his debt to Harnack: "What I have learned and understood in your seminar is too closely bound to my entire person for me to ever forget it."[4]

Bonhoeffer attended numerous events held by the Luther scholar Karl Holl and wrote several seminar papers on Luther for him. Next to Karl Barth, Luther is the theologian who had the greatest influence on Bonhoeffer's own thought. Bonhoeffer's criticisms of Barth are often closely connected to that influence, since Luther stressed God's presence in the humanity of Jesus Christ more strongly than did the Reformed theologian Barth. Bonhoeffer wrote his dissertation, however, under Reinhold Seeberg, a historian of dogma and systematic theologian. Under Seeberg Bonhoeffer was able to pursue his interest in writing a "half-historical and half-systematic" work on the church.[5]

The Community of Saints

Bonhoeffer chose the church as the subject for his doctoral work. By the age of twenty-one he had completed his study, *Sanctorum Communio: Eine dogmatische Untersuchung zur Soziologie der Kirche* [ET: *Sanctorum Communio: A Theological Study of the Sociology of the Church*]; it was published in 1930. In it Bonhoeffer focuses on the sociality—that is, the fundamental social orientation—of human beings and of Christian faith. Bonhoeffer was convinced that we human beings are not characterized primarily by the fact that we are autonomous, rational beings in the sense of the Enlightenment. It is much more the case that we are beings who are truly human only when in our encounter with another we recognize our responsibility toward the other. Put differently: we human beings recognize who we are only in the encounter with another person, when we are confronted with a concrete You who demands our help and attention. In this moment the human being becomes a person.

If the human being is at the core a social being, then social existence must also be an indispensable aspect of being a Christian. Bonhoeffer is convinced that one cannot be a Christian just for oneself, but always only in the community of the faithful, in the *communio sanctorum*, the community of the

---

4. DBWE 9:439.
5. DBWE 9:148.

saints. Even more: only in faith do human beings grasp the full extent of their fundamental social nature, for in faith a completely new orientation in human existence is carried out. While the lives of human beings in sin only revolve around themselves and they stand in a relationship to other human beings that is purely demanding, in faith they are free from this self-centeredness and open for the other. This is not a theological ideal; rather, according to Bonhoeffer, this happens very concretely wherever human beings exist together as church, which means to celebrate worship together, be there for one another, pray for others, and forgive one another's sins. Church is where Christians realize the fact that they all already stand in a fellowship with each other through their faith in Christ.

In his work on the community structure of the church Bonhoeffer used sociological methods, which at that time were new. He utilized the concepts of academic sociology to describe the gathering of human beings in the church. Nonetheless, he was convinced that the reality of church is not exhausted in sociological, that is, empirically noticeable, categories. The church can be described as a historical fellowship with sociological means, but it is "simultaneously . . . established by God."[6] The basis for human beings belonging together in the church is not their similar interests or a need for community but God, for through the relationship of each individual believer to Jesus Christ, the believers stand in relationship to one another. Bonhoeffer later put it this way: "Christian community means community through Jesus Christ and in Jesus Christ."[7] At the same time, Christ is present in Christian community. Bonhoeffer thereby coined the famous formula: the church is "Christ existing as community."[8] Jesus Christ is encountered by human beings in the church, in the sermon and sacraments, and in the neighbor in whose love I encounter Christ. For those who do not live in Jesus' times—that is, for us—there is no longer any other possibility of encountering Christ today.

It was already evident in his dissertation that Bonhoeffer in the meantime had discovered the theology of Karl Barth. Starting in the 1924/25 winter semester he followed avidly the new theological thinking of this father of so-called dialectical theology. Shortly before this, in 1922, Barth had launched a furor among theological faculties and in parsonages through the second edition of his *The Epistle to the Romans*. Here was someone who criticized all the

---

6. DBWE 1:126.
7. DBWE 5:31.
8. E.g., in DBWE 1:141.

theology of that era because in it "the *human being* is made great at the cost of *God*."[9] The error of contemporary theology, according to Barth, is that it speaks in high praise of human religion and its cultural power, rather than of God. Human religion, however, can never reach God because there exists an "infinitely qualitative difference" between God and the human.[10] God must disclose Godself to human beings to be recognized; God must reveal Godself. Even then God cannot be in human hands; God is not at our disposal. Bonhoeffer was convinced by Barth's distinction between religion and revelation, and he was fascinated by Barth's thesis that theology's task is to speak of God and that its starting point is the church sermon. Nonetheless, in his postdoctoral thesis he would criticize Barth's one-sided emphasis on God's freedom.

"What Is Better: School or Vacation?"

As he began work on his dissertation Bonhoeffer also helped in the Sunday school at the church in Grunewald; this was a requirement for his first theological examination. His sermons from that time are direct and emotional, attempting to connect to the world as children experience it. He begins a homily about the Ten Commandments as follows: "All of you can answer my first question. What is better: school or vacation? Are there a few upstanding students who would really say that school is better? Oh no, I don't think so."[11] From there he leads the children to consider the difference between freedom and coercion, so that they might see that for those who gladly do what is commanded, coercion is at the same time freedom. In this way the children are to understand that the Ten Commandments don't restrict them but, rather, are easy to follow for those who love God.

Evidently Bonhoeffer was beloved by the children in Grunewald. Several of them continued to meet with him in spring 1927 in a youth circle where they discussed political, cultural, and theological questions and visited musical performances together.

---

9. Karl Barth, *Die Menschlichkeit Gottes* (Zollikon-Zurich: Theologischer Verlag, 1956), 5 [ET: *The Humanity of God*].
10. Karl Barth, *Römerbrief*, 2d ed. (Zurich: Theologischer Verlag, 1922), 73 [ET: *The Epistle to the Romans*].
11. DBWE 9:456.

CHAPTER THREE

WIDER HORIZONS, 1928–1931

For a young man of his generation, Bonhoeffer gained an extraordinary amount of experience abroad. After completing his dissertation he spent one year as a vicar in a German overseas congregation in Barcelona; two years later he studied for two semesters at Union Theological Seminary in New York.

Bonhoeffer's Time as Vicar in Barcelona

Bonhoeffer arrived in Barcelona in February 1928. Berlin church superintendent Max Diestel had offered him an opportunity to do his training as vicar in the German congregation there. Bonhoeffer was already feeling the desire to move beyond the familiar and become truly independent, but he discussed it first with his parents. As he later wrote in his diary in Spain, "the issue decided itself."[1] As Bonhoeffer himself observed, it was often the case that he didn't reach clear decisions on a matter; rather, clarity about a decision gradually grew within him, more instinctively and less an intellectual choice.

---

1. DBWE 10:57.

For Bonhoeffer the period in Barcelona, as he later wrote, would be his "first encounter . . . with ecumenical Christianity."[2] For the first time it became clear to him that the scope of the Christian church was worldwide, not just national—an insight that several years later would set the course for his engagement in the ecumenical movement, his peace activism, and his critique of the ethno-nationalist mentality of the German Christians. During his year as vicar he broadened his cultural horizons through numerous trips through Spain, to Madrid, Mallorca, Morocco, and Andalusia.

Parish work, however, was not easy. He got along well enough with his mentoring pastor, Friedrich Olbricht, and to some extent the two men even liked each other. Yet, as Bonhoeffer finally noted in his diary, they essentially remained strangers, and he reported in letters that there was a certain sense of competition between them. After Bonhoeffer was introduced to the congregation, for example, the previously poorly attended church services began to draw more parishioners when Bonhoeffer was preaching. Olbricht in turn stopped giving advance notice of who the preacher on Sunday would be. Drawing on his experiences in Berlin, Bonhoeffer also built up a well-attended Sunday school for the congregation's children.

The congregation also had a charitable ministry for Germans in Barcelona who had fallen on hard times. The tough economic situation of the 1920s had hit many of those who came in for help. Bonhoeffer's letters show that he had some difficulty with this part of his job:

> While the pastor was away, I had to hold office hours for the relief agency alone from 9:00 to 11:00 A.M. That usually doesn't make for a very pleasant start to my day—though it is always very instructive and interesting. People continually lie to you—which you learn only later—and there is rarely a case when you really are glad to help and can do so with a good conscience, and that's really too bad.[3]

Through this work, however, Bonhoeffer developed an unusual openness for a wide range of people, and he learned to distinguish between those who call themselves Christians and those who actually are—a gift that would become even more evident during his later imprisonment:

---

2. DBWE 16:367.
3. DBWE 10:89.

. . . one encounters people here the way they are, far from the masquerade of the "Christian world"; people with passions, criminal types, small people with small goals, small drives, and small crimes—all in all, people who feel homeless in both senses, people who thaw a bit when you speak to them in a friendly manner—real people. I can only say I have the impression that precisely these people stand more under grace than under wrath, but that it is precisely the Christian world that stands more under wrath than under grace. "I am sought out by those who did not ask; . . . to those who did not call on my name I said, 'Here I am'" (Isa 65:1).[4]

In addition to preaching regularly, Bonhoeffer gave several lectures. To some extent these revealed the unbowed pathos of a young man, but there was also evidence of fundamental theological decisions that would later have great significance for him. In a lecture about the Old Testament prophets Bonhoeffer sternly warned his audience, in light of the destabilization brought about through the First World War and the difficult economic and social situation in Europe:

Our own age is getting out of joint. The vital force of our people, of Europe, seems broken. The hideous face of decadence, of immorality, of cynicism, of depravity grins at us from every corner and every crevice. In the face of such developments, one must embrace simplicity again, and for that reason we have listened once more to the words of the ancient prophets. They said it then and could not have said it better: a people who would rise up must be serious about God's will and must be serious about a life of morality. All the blows of fate that come upon a people are both justified and merited, for it is God who has sent them. The point now is to draw the appropriate conclusions from such blows and to bear them as a burden that God lays upon us.[5]

In a lecture about Jesus Christ and the nature of Christianity Bonhoeffer referred for the first time to the distinction between religion and Christian faith, which he had learned from the theology of Karl Barth. This distinction would remain relevant for Bonhoeffer's theology even as its shape became

---

4. DBWE 10:127.
5. DBWE 10:341.

more his own. In the Barcelona lecture, however, he completely followed Barth. While, for Bonhoeffer, religion is the human attempt to find one's own way to God, the beginning of Christian faith is God's path to human beings through Jesus Christ:

> . . . from the perspective of human initiative, this chasm [between God and humanity] remains unbridgeable. Human knowledge of God remains precisely that: human, limited, relative, anthropomorphic knowledge. The human desire to believe remains precisely that: human desire accompanied by ultimately human goals and motives. The human religious path to God leads to the idol of our own hearts, which we have created in our own image. . . . If human beings and God are to come together, there is but one way, namely, the way from God to human beings.[6]

In the same lecture Bonhoeffer drew a further distinction that from then on would remain fundamental: the difference between a system or principle, on the one hand, and concrete existence in history, on the other. Whoever approaches reality with a finished system, or thinks that they can address reality through general principles and rules, will be incapable of truly perceiving reality. Instead, they will only discover and rediscover their own previously formed intellectual image of reality. In contrast, whoever is open to the concrete situation in which they find themselves, open to the contingencies and unpredictability of history, will discover that while their fixed ideas and opinions may be shattered, the reality will do them good.

A third parish lecture in Barcelona, "Basic Questions of a Christian Ethic," again took up the distinction between principle and the concrete: ". . . there are not and cannot be Christian norms and principles of a moral nature. Only in the actual execution of a given action do the concepts of 'good' and 'bad' apply, that is, only in the given present moment; hence any attempt to explicate principles is like trying to draw a bird in flight."[7] For when human beings could base their behavior on principles and rules, then "there could be ethical action without any immediate relationship with God."[8] Christians could then no longer ask themselves what the good thing in that situation would be from

6. DBWE 10:353.
7. DBWE 10:360.
8. DBWE 10:366.

God's perspective but, instead, could direct themselves, utterly independent of God, toward the good. At the same time, however, they would no longer be acting freely and responsibly, but would become the slave of their principles.

Even if these reflections are easily comprehensible, Bonhoeffer's lecture on ethics includes statements that for readers today are intolerable. To the question of whether a Christian should go to war or not, Bonhoeffer wrote that in the "distressing situation of having to decide,"

> . . . the moment itself will doubtless tell me which of these two is and must be my neighbor, including before the eyes of God. God gave me my mother, my people. For what I have, I thank my people; what I am, I am through my people, and so what I have should also belong to my people; that is in the divine order of things, for God created the peoples . . . love for my people will sanctify murder, will sanctify war. As a Christian, I will suffer from the entire dreadfulness of war. My soul will bear the entire burden of responsibility in its full gravity. I will try to love my enemies against whom I am sworn to the death, as only Christians can love their brothers. And yet I will have to do to those enemies what my love and gratitude toward my own people command me to do, the people into whom God bore me.[9]

Not long afterward Bonhoeffer himself energetically refuted these opinions in the context of his ecumenical engagement.

As he wrote to a friend, Bonhoeffer's new church, social, and political experiences in Barcelona led him "to see work and life genuinely converge—a synthesis that we all sought but rarely found in our student days—when one really lives *one* life rather than two, or better: half a life; it lends dignity to the work and objectivity to the worker, and a recognition of one's own limitations of the sort acquired only within concrete life."[10] Bonhoeffer now saw that "one really finds oneself forced to reassess one's theology from the ground up."[11] In fact, this emerged as a feature of his theology in general: new political, social, church, or even personal situations would lead him to reevaluate his previous theological positions.

---

9. DBWE 10:372.
10. DBWE 10:126.
11. DBWE 10:76.

Assistantship in Berlin

After his return from Spain in February 1929 Bonhoeffer decided to prepare for his second theological examination. At the same time he was working on a postdoctoral dissertation, in order to have the qualifications to apply for a professorship. He was exempted from attending the required preachers' seminary when he received a post as an adjunct assistant to Wilhelm Lütgert, the New Testament and systematics scholar at the University of Berlin. During his time in Barcelona he had thoroughly revised his dissertation for publication and was thinking of a new academic topic. In July 1928 he wrote Reinhold Seeberg: "At the same time my thoughts are already busy with another project, albeit again not historical but rather systematic. It picks up the question of consciousness and conscience in theology . . . but this will be a theological study rather than a psychological one."[12]

In fact, the work that Bonhoeffer submitted to the theological faculty in Berlin in March 1930 focused on the question of how to conceptualize the particular epistemology of faith, in contrast to philosophical epistemology. In September 1931 this was published as *Akt und Sein: Transzendentalphilosophie und Ontologie in der systematischen Theologie* [ET: *Act and Being: Transcendental Philosophy and Ontology in Systematic Theology*].

As had been the case with his dissertation, there was little academic reaction to this volume. It was a densely written study in which Bonhoeffer articulated how to conceptualize revelation and the believer precisely, in conversation with contemporary philosophical and theological approaches. Was revelation—that is, God's communication with and attention to human beings—something that only happens now and then, therefore always being withdrawn from humans, and for that reason human faith can only exist in concrete acts but never be truly perceived? Is the relationship between revelation and the believer only an occasional event, with no lasting character or continuity? Or is God's attention to the human person something that we find as a given, something that is always at our disposal at a certain place and which we can therefore relate to in a lasting sense? Can revelation and the believer therefore each be conceived of as having a continuous, persisting character?

Bonhoeffer concluded that both these views were incorrect. The first case overlooks the fact that God, in the divine turn toward human beings, has

---

12. DBWE 10:122.

located and bound Godself in Jesus Christ. The second case understands this location in Christ as if God had made Godself fully available to the human being and therefore no longer challenges people in any meaningful way. Whereas the first criticism was directed primarily at Karl Barth, the second was directed primarily at certain forms of Catholic theology.

Bonhoeffer states his own view that revelation and belief can neither be understood purely as act nor purely as being. The structure of revelation is suspended between act and being, namely, in the church as the community of those who believe in Christ. Here Christ always encounters us concretely in the sermon, in the sacraments, and in the other believers; he has bound himself to this place. At the same time, Christ is not simply available in the church, because these forms of encounter demand something of us that challenges our very self-understanding.

Bonhoeffer summed up his central insights from *Act and Being* in his inaugural lecture at the University of Berlin on July 31, 1930. The title of the lecture was "The Anthropological Question in Contemporary Philosophy and Theology." With that, his postdoctoral qualification process was finished.

A Student in New York

Bonhoeffer's time in New York would have an even greater influence on him than the year in Barcelona. Once more with the support of Max Diestel, after he completed his second theological examination Bonhoeffer received a scholarship from the German Academic Exchange Service for a year of study at Union Theological Seminary. He departed by ship for the United States on September 5, 1930. After a short stay with distant relatives in Philadelphia he arrived at the seminary, which is located in Manhattan between the Upper West Side and Harlem. Union Theological Seminary at the time was the pinnacle of American liberal theology.

Bonhoeffer's first impressions were sobering. He wrote Max Diestel:

First of all, life at the seminary is quite stimulating and instructive as far as the personal contacts, which are also quite cordial with the professors themselves. . . . One almost has to be cautious lest the mutual visits and chatting take up too much time. For—these conversations almost never yield anything of substance. And that brings me to the sad part of the whole thing. There is no theology here. Although I am basically taking classes and lectures in dogmatics and philosophy of religion, the impression is overwhelmingly negative. They talk a blue streak without the slightest substantive foundation and with no evidence of any criteria. . . . It often just burns me up when people here deal with Christ and are then done with him, and laugh insolently if someone presents a citation from Luther on the consciousness of guilt. . . . Despite all this, I am nonetheless grateful to have been so thoroughly introduced to these basic questions again. Indeed, here one once again understands what important questions really are and how much one owes to our own theology.[13]

He was also initially disappointed by the church landscape in the United States, writing that the sermons he heard were more commentaries on current events than true proclamation:

In New York, they preach about virtually everything; only one thing is not addressed, or is addressed so rarely that I have as yet been unable to hear it, namely, the gospel of Jesus Christ, the cross, sin and forgiveness, death and life. . . . So what stands in place of the Christian message? An ethical and social idealism borne by a faith in progress that—who knows how—claims the right to call itself "Christian" . . . some churches are basically "charitable" churches; others have primarily a social identity. One cannot avoid the impression, however, that in both cases they have forgotten what the real point is.[14]

Bonhoeffer was also confronted in New York with his identity as a German, and was invited to give several political talks so that people could find out how Germany was thinking about a possible new war. In his talks about the German situation he reassured his listeners and described with some sadness how the First World War had brought death to almost every German family. Although he rejected the notion of Germany's sole responsibility for the war, he described it as the expression of God's wrath toward the guilt of the German people, for through this war people had become distant from God, believing too much in their own power and right. For the first time in these

---

13. DBWE 10:265–66; trans. altered.
14. DBWE 10:313–14.

Dietrich Bonhoeffer (no. 12) at Union Theological Seminary 1930/31

talks Bonhoeffer argued using a peace ethic: never again could it happen that Christian peoples fought against one another, for they had the same Father. Christians lived in a worldwide unity, beyond national interests.

Bonhoeffer's theological talks during this period reveal a man who identified more strongly with the theology of Karl Barth than he had in his postdoctoral dissertation. In light of the rejection or ignorance of Barthianism he discovered at Union, his critique of Barth in *Act and Being* now began to move into the background.

Yet it appears that Bonhoeffer enjoyed living together with his fellow seminarians. He noted that it produced a strong spirit of helpful camaraderie, but he was critical when, for the sake of that fellowship, someone avoided conflict by avoiding the truth about something—a criticism that he would later also make in the German Church Struggle. He quickly became close friends with several fellow students whose friendship altered his theology.

One of these friends was Frank Fisher, an African American student whose family Bonhoeffer visited during the winter break, where he got to know several leading African Americans. He wrote his parents:

In Washington I lived completely among the Negroes and through the students was able to become acquainted with all the leading figures of the Negro movement, was in their homes, and had extraordinarily interesting discussions with them. . . . The conditions are really rather unbelievable. Not just separate railway cars, tramways, and buses south of Washington, but also, for example, when I wanted to eat in a small restaurant with a Negro, I was refused service.[15]

As his friends introduced him to the difficult circumstances that African Americans faced, Bonhoeffer witnessed the evils of racist ideology for the first time: "The way the southerners talk about the Negroes is simply repugnant, and in this regard the pastors are no better than the others. . . . It is a bit unnerving that in a country with so inordinately many slogans about brotherhood, peace, and so on, such things still continue completely uncorrected."[16] At the same time, he experienced a "greater religious power and originality"[17] among African Americans that inspired him. He read novels by young black writers with fascination, and he actively participated in the life of Abyssinian Baptist Church in Harlem, teaching Sunday school and holding women's Bible studies, sometimes together with Frank Fisher and sometimes by himself. Parishioners often invited him to their homes. In his final report about the time in New York he noted that he had heard the gospel preached in the black church. His personal encounters with African Americans had been one of "the most important and gratifying events" of his time on the other side of the Atlantic.[18]

Another important seminary friend was the Calvinist French minister Jean Lasserre, who was a fellow student at Union that year. A movie screening of the film *All Quiet on the Western Front* was decisive for both men, who were deeply disturbed by the audience applause when a German killed a French soldier. They sensed that, despite their different backgrounds, they were united by the same Christian faith. Lasserre later said that both began to become pacifists in that moment, and presumably Bonhoeffer's reorientation around the Sermon on the Mount, which began after his return from the United States, also had its roots in this experience. But while Lasserre decided on a principled

15. DBWE 10:258.
16. DBWE 10:269.
17. DBWE 10:266.
18. DBWE 10:315.

pacifism and interpreted the Sermon on the Mount from this perspective, Bonhoeffer's peace ethics was grounded in the concrete discipleship to Christ. Both would continue the relationship after the year at Union through their ecumenical activities. First, however, they traveled together to Mexico in 1931 to visit the theological seminary and German congregations there.

An American doctoral student, Paul Lehmann, was one of the few in the New York seminary who was interested in the theology of Karl Barth; as a result, Bonhoeffer could discuss theology with him in more depth than with others. In 1932 Lehmann spent a year in Zurich and Bonn studying under Emil Brunner and Karl Barth. Lehmann and Bonhoeffer met again in Berlin in the spring of 1933 before Lehmann's return to the United States, and in 1939 he was one of those who helped organize Bonhoeffer's second U.S. trip. Lehmann would later incorporate many of Bonhoeffer's theological insights into his own publications.

Finally, a Swiss student named Erwin Sutz became a friend. Bonhoeffer traveled with him to Cuba over the 1930 Christmas break, where they stayed with a sister of Bonhoeffer's childhood governess, Maria Horn, who worked at the German school in Havana. Bonhoeffer gave two sermons in the German parish there.

Even at the end of his study year Bonhoeffer remained skeptical of the American theology of the time. In April 1931 he reported to his grandmother about a conference of leading systematic theologians. The discussions had been so unsatisfying, "really almost like discussions among students in their first semesters, that I am still quite depressed."[19]

Nonetheless, it was not only his friendships but the American academic debates that gave Bonhoeffer impulses for new ideas that would later be fruitful for his own theology in Germany. His personal study under Professor Eugene William Lyman on contemporary American philosophy was important, focusing particularly on pragmatism (William James, John Dewey, Bertrand Russell, and others). Bonhoeffer viewed pragmatism critically to the extent that it oriented truth in terms of its practical applications, but at the same time he was fascinated to discover its concept of God. God is not only "valid" truth but "effective" truth: ". . . he is either active in the processes of human life or he 'is' not at all."[20] Although Bonhoeffer sensed the danger that this rendered

---

19. DBWE 10:295–96.
20. DBWE 10:311.

God dependent on human beings, he later took this up in *Ethics* (without succumbing to this danger) in terms of the thought that truth alters reality.

In addition, in the lectures of Reinhold Niebuhr and Harry Ward, Bonhoeffer became familiar with the "social gospel" and its direct application of the Christian gospel to immediate social issues. Here, too, Bonhoeffer complained about the lack of interest in theological reflection and the Bible. At the same time, it made a lasting impression on him to see how seriously the social gospel theology took social, economic, and political difficulties. Many of the fundamental ideas he encountered here, such as the emphasis on the Ten Commandments, the Sermon on the Mount, and the kingdom of God, became significant in his own thought. In his final report on the year at Union he noted that the impression he had received from the advocates of the social gospel would "remain determinative for me for a long time to come."[21] One year after he had returned from the United States he expressed his appreciation for this line of thought:

> The unrelenting seriousness with which the practical social problems are shown here, and with which Christians are called on to serve, is the decisive contribution of American Christians to the understanding of the Christian message in the entire world. The personal and sober passion of those involved in the social gospel demand a decision of everyone who comes into contact with it.[22]

---

21. DBWE 10:318.
22. DBWE 12:241.

CHAPTER FOUR

BEGINNINGS, 1931–1932

Bonhoeffer's Encounter with Karl Barth

Before taking up his new duties as student chaplain at the Technical College in Berlin Bonhoeffer traveled to Bonn for three weeks in 1931 so that he could finally meet Karl Barth. Barth had been professor of systematic theology there since 1930. Bonhoeffer visited the seminar and graduate seminar; Barth also invited him to his home. Bonhoeffer wrote to his friend Erwin Sutz, enthusiastically describing Barth's way of doing theology:

> I have, I believe, seldom regretted not having done something in my theological past as much as I now regret that I did not go to hear Barth sooner. . . . it is important and surprising in the nicest way to see how Barth continues to think beyond his books. There is an openness, a willingness to listen to a critical comment directed to the topic at hand, and with this such concentration and with a vehement insistence on the topic at hand. . . . It is becoming easier and easier for me to understand why it is unbelievably difficult to grasp Barth through the literature. I am impressed by his discussion even more than by his writing and lectures. He is really fully present. I have never seen anything like it nor thought

it possible. . . . This is really someone from whom one could learn something, and there one sits in poor, desolate Berlin and is discouraged because there is no one there from whom one can learn theology and some other useful things along with it.[1]

Out of this first personal encounter something almost like a friendship developed between the older and the younger theologian. Each attentively followed the other's publications, and even in prison Bonhoeffer asked to be sent the publisher's galleys of the second part of volume 2 of Barth's *Church Dogmatics*. At key points in his life Bonhoeffer sought Barth's advice, both personally and with respect to church politics. Again and again he also longed for a personal conversation, particularly later during the period of political resistance. It gave him a sense of reverent delight when Barth sent him a cigar in Tegel prison.

First Ecumenical Engagement

At the urging of his mentor, Max Diestel, Bonhoeffer participated in the September 1931 meeting of what was then called the World Alliance for Promoting International Friendship through the Churches in Cambridge, as well as the preparatory youth conference at the end of August. The World Alliance was one of the most important ecumenical organizations of that era, and its emphasis on social and practical issues found a wide resonance among Christians and local congregations. At the meeting Bonhoeffer was elected to be one of three international youth secretaries for the World Alliance, so he immediately became a member of its executive council.

Yet the World Alliance's situation was not easy. It was in financial difficulties because of the worldwide economic crisis and, particularly among the younger generation, intensifying nationalism was leading to contempt for the efforts toward an international ecumenism among Protestants. Some of Bonhoeffer's contemporaries viewed such ecumenical engagement as a betrayal of the political realities of the time. For example, the Luther scholars Paul Althaus and Emanuel Hirsch both announced in advance of a preparatory conference for the Cambridge meeting to be held in Hamburg that in light of these current ecumenical efforts it would be important "to break through all the artificial illusions of fellowship and acknowledge without reservation that

---

1. DBWE 11:37–38, trans. altered.

Christian and ecclesial understanding and cooperation around questions of bringing the nations together is impossible as long as the others are carrying out murderous policies aimed against our people."[2]

Bonhoeffer's perspective had changed markedly since his time in the United States and his experience there of a connectedness through Christian faith that transcended national boundaries. He was of the opinion that "the church alone can be the foundation on which the international discussion, otherwise so dubious, can be conducted openly and objectively . . . for many it was overwhelming to listen to the other who is so different, to see and simply allow him first of all just to be as he is, and from that perspective then to rediscover themselves."[3]

In addition to his work in the Berlin Provisional Bureau that coordinated the German ecumenical youth work, Bonhoeffer attended numerous ecumenical meetings as a youth secretary of the World Alliance. His July 1932 talk at the World Alliance international youth meeting in Ciernohorské Kúpele in Czechoslovakia has become famous. Bonhoeffer's talk was based on his impression that people in ecumenical work relied too easily on feelings of friendship and that the ecumenical movement lacked a theological foundation. Bonhoeffer attempted to offer such a foundation by elaborating on the concept that the ecumenical movement was a particular form of church. Only the worldwide ecumenical movement could express that the church's proclamation was aimed for the entire world, going beyond the scope of the national church bodies.

Bonhoeffer raised key questions: How should this worldwide proclamation be conceived? What should be the nature of church statements on current political, social, and ethical questions, and how should they be reached? How in particular should the church speak to the question of peace?

For Bonhoeffer, the church's task was not to assert general rules for life or principled ethical norms. The church was to formulate a concrete ethical commandment with regard to the contemporary situation. Before making a statement on something it had the obligation to acquire thorough competence on the issue. Bonhoeffer's demand for concreteness was based on his opinion that God always calls human beings to very specific and concrete deeds, and that the task of the church's proclamation is to make this clear:

---

2. Paul Althaus and Emanuel Hirsch, „Evangelische Kirche und Völkerverständigung," *Die Christliche Welt* 45 (1931): 606.
3. DBWE 11:385.

> The church . . . can proclaim not principles that are always true but rather only commandments that are true today. For that which is "always" true is precisely not true "today": God is for us "always" *God* precisely "*today*" . . . the commandment: "Love thy neighbor" is as such so general, that it requires the strongest concretion if I am to hear what it means for me here and today. And only as such a concrete word to me is it God's word.[4]

Only when the church can speak concretely in this way should it address political questions: "The church must in the event of a decision about war not only be able to say: There should be no war; but there are also necessary wars, and then leave it to each individual to apply this principle—rather, the church should be able to say concretely: fight this war, or do not fight this war."[5] Bonhoeffer believed that in the contemporary situation the church, as it is realized in ecumenism, had to speak concretely, for it had acknowledged a very specific commandment of God for that situation: the cause of international peace. It wasn't a matter of peace at any cost; if peace endangered truth and justice, then one must fight for a better peace. But in the situation of the times such a fight could no longer mean war. For—according to Bonhoeffer's judgment after the experience of a world war—war today would mean "the certain self-destruction of both warring sides . . . [for that reason] today's war, the next war, must be *condemned* by the church."[6]

Bonhoeffer explicitly stressed that he did not want to claim that the commandment "Thou shalt not kill" ultimately had a higher value than the others. He held such a general repudiation of violence to be "Enthusiastic."[7] Yet the church had to repudiate the next war, since in light of the military potential for extermination God's commandment was that there should be no more war.

First Pastorate

On November 15, 1931, Bonhoeffer was ordained in St. Matthew's Church in Berlin. As part of his assistantship as City Vicar in Berlin he had been assigned to the newly created office of student chaplain at the Technical College in

---

4. DBWE 11:359–60.
5. DBWE 11:360.
6. DBWE 11:366–67.
7. "Enthusiasm" (German: *Schwärmertum*) was Luther's (and later Bonhoeffer's) critical description of the Anabaptists and the radical Reformation movement; DBWE 11:365.

Charlottenburg. He was primarily to take care of pastoral counseling but he also organized prayers and lectures. None of these found much resonance among the students.

He also had been assigned with teaching confirmation students at the Zion Church in central Berlin. At first the work was not easy; it was a group of some fifty undisciplined youths: "That is about the toughest neighborhood of Berlin, with the most difficult socioeconomic and political conditions. At the beginning the boys were acting wild, so for the first time I really had discipline problems. But here too one thing helped, namely, just simply telling the boys Bible stories in all their intensity. . . . Now it is absolutely quiet . . ."[8] Bonhoeffer took outings with the youths and even moved closer to the church so that they could visit him during the evenings for homework or games. He also visited their families and was shocked by their impoverished conditions. Yet during these visits it was extraordinarily difficult for him to talk with them about their pastoral needs.

Dietrich Bonhoeffer with a group of confirmands in 1932

---

8. DBWE 11:76; trans. altered.

Bonhoeffer involved his confirmation pupils in the preparations for the final confirmation service. At the end of his time with them he took a group out to the weekend country home his family owned in Friedrichsbrunn. Filled with the success of the trip, he wrote his parents:

> I am very happy that I can be up here with the confirmands. Even if they don't have much understanding of the woods and nature, they are enthusiastic about climbing excursions in the Bodetal and soccer in the meadow. . . . I believe, too, that later you won't see any changes to the house to show that these people have been here. Except for one broken windowpane, everything is still intact.[9]

In the fall of 1932, inspired by the social work he had seen in New York and with the financial help of Anneliese Schnurmann, a friend of his sister Susanne, Bonhoeffer opened a club for unemployed youth in Charlottenburg. This work ended rapidly in January 1933 when Hitler came to power, since Schnurmann was Jewish and had to leave Germany quickly—and the communist youths who visited his club could no longer be certain they wouldn't be attacked physically by storm troopers or other Nazi party members.

First Lectures at the University

In August 1931, in addition to his pastoral activities, Bonhoeffer also received an assistantship at his alma mater in Berlin. He began teaching there as a lecturer. During the winter semester of 1931/32, he taught a seminar on the relationship between theology and philosophy as well as a lecture course on the history of twentieth-century systematic theology, in which he again showed his critical closeness to the theology of Karl Barth. This was followed by a lecture course in the summer of 1932 on "The Nature of the Church" as well as a seminar on whether there was a Christian ethic. His lectures on the church took up a number of ideas from *Sanctorum Communio* and *Act and Being*, and the seminar focused on the question that had already become important for him about the possibility of hearing God's commandment in a concrete situation. In his lecture course during the 1932/33 winter semester he focused on new publications in systematic theology and a course in theological psychology in which he also incorporated insights from *Act and Being*.

---

9. DBWE 11:109.

His 1932/33 lectures on "creation and sin" reached a larger audience in their 1933 publication as *Schöpfung und Fall* [ET: *Creation and Fall*]. In this work Bonhoeffer offered a unique interpretation of Genesis 1–3, the first three chapters in the Bible, which tell of God's creation of the world, the fall into sin, and banishment from paradise. While he wanted to analyze the biblical text linguistically and historically, Bonhoeffer also wanted to go beyond these usual methods of the time: whoever deals with the Bible theologically, he wrote, needs to interpret it as the "book of the church."[10] This meant that the Bible has to be read from the perspective of Christian faith. Bonhoeffer therefore renarrated the Old Testament texts, which had been written from the perspective of Jewish faith, from the perspective of the Christian understanding of God. This is particularly evident in his description of the creation of human beings:

> To say that in humankind God creates the image of God on earth means
> that humankind is like the Creator in that it is free. . . . For in the

Dietrich Bonhoeffer with students from Berlin in 1932

10. DBWE 3:22.

language of the Bible freedom is not something that people have for themselves but something they have for others. . . . Being free means "being-free-for-the-other." . . . We can ask how we know this. . . . The answer is that it is the message of the Gospel [of Jesus Christ] itself that God's freedom has bound itself to us, that God's free grace becomes real with us alone, that God wills not to be free for God's self but for humankind.[11]

For Bonhoeffer, the similarity between God and the human person exists precisely in this relation to the other in freedom. Yet while God is not dependent on the other, but comes into relationship with human beings only because God wants to, the human being is indeed dependent upon the other. The human person needs God and the other human person in order to be human.

Bonhoeffer's graphic description of the fall is impressive. As soon as the humans listen to the serpent's question, "Did God really say . . . ?," they abandon the appropriate attitude toward God. Now the human being begins to "sit in judgment on God's word instead of simply listening to it and doing it."[12] The serpent continues: yes, God said that humans should not eat from the tree of knowledge of good and evil, for then humans will be able to judge for themselves between good and evil. But: "God said it out of envy. . . . God is not a good but an evil, cruel God; be clever, be cleverer than your God and take what God begrudges you. . . ."[13] Consequently, when human beings eat of the forbidden fruit they transgress the boundary God has set for them. From now on they experience all their boundaries, including those set by other human beings, as unjust limitations and fight them. Bonhoeffer declares that conscience, which modernity praises as an example of self-determination, is the result of the fall: here human beings have become their own judge, rather than opening themselves to the judgment of God. The human being cannot go back to a time before the fall, but now lives in a world marked by sin.

Bonhoeffer was not particularly comfortable on the Berlin theological faculty. "My theological origin is gradually becoming suspect here, and they seem to have somewhat the feeling that they have been nurturing a viper in their bosom."[14] But among the students he quickly developed a following,

---

11. DBWE 3:62–63.
12. DBWE 3:108.
13. DBWE 3:112.
14. DBWE 11:76.

from which a circle of students emerged who met regularly with Bonhoeffer for evening discussions and excursions, even on the weekends. Several of those who later helped in Finkenwalde and stood with him in the Church Struggle came from this circle, including Otto Dudzus, Herbert Jehle, Joachim Kanitz, Winfried Maechler, Albrecht Schönherr, Jürgen Winterhager, and Wolf-Dieter Zimmermann.

"For the First Time, I Came to the Bible"

In a January 1936 letter to his friend Elisabeth Zinn, Bonhoeffer reported of an existential change that had taken place before 1933; the exact date and the cause are still debated. Bonhoeffer wrote that it was through turning to the Bible that he had first truly become a Christian and understood what it meant to be a pastor:

> I threw myself into my work in an extremely un-Christian and not at all humble fashion. A rather crazy element of ambition, which some people noticed in me, made my life difficult and withdrew from me the love and trust of those around me. At that time, I was terribly alone and left to myself. It was quite bad. But then something different came, something that has changed and transformed my life to this very day. For the first time, I came to the Bible. That, too, is an awful thing to say. I had often preached, I had seen a great deal of the church, had spoken and written about it—and yet I was not yet a Christian but rather in an utterly wild and uncontrolled fashion my own master. I do know that at the time I turned the cause of Jesus Christ into an advantage for myself, for my crazy vanity. I pray to God that will never happen again. Nor had I ever prayed, or had done so only very rarely. Despite this isolation, I was quite happy with myself. The Bible, especially the Sermon on the Mount, freed me from all this. Since then everything has changed. I have felt this plainly and so have other people around me. That was a great liberation. It became clear to me that the life of a servant of Jesus Christ must belong to the church, and step by step it became clearer to me how far it must go. Then came the crisis of 1933. This strengthened me in it. I also met others who shared the same goal. For me everything now depended on a renewal of the church and of the pastoral station. . . . Christian pacifism, which a brief time before I had still passionately disputed, suddenly

came into focus as something utterly self-evident. And thus it went, step by step. I no longer saw or thought about anything else.[15]

During the 1930s regular reflection and an orientation toward the Bible became increasingly important for Bonhoeffer. At a 1932 ecumenical meeting in the Swiss town of Gland he critically warned his audience: ". . . has it not become terribly clear, again and again, in all that we have discussed with one another here, that we are no longer obedient to the Bible? We prefer our own thoughts to those of the Bible. We no longer read the Bible seriously. We read it no longer against ourselves but only for ourselves."[16] In the years that followed Bonhoeffer would make this assessment repeatedly: one treats the biblical text incorrectly if it is used only to confirm one's own behavior rather than calling that into question. He, too, wanted to allow himself to be challenged through the Bible. Bonhoeffer reflects on this haunting quest in a biographical note found in an April 1936 letter to his brother-in-law Rüdiger Schleicher:

One cannot simply *read* the Bible like other books. One must be prepared genuinely to query it. . . . The reason is that God is speaking to us in the Bible. And one cannot simply reflect on God on one's own; one must ask God. . . . Every other place outside the Bible has become too uncertain for me. There I am always afraid of encountering merely my own divine Doppelgänger [look-alike].[17]

15. DBWE 14:134.
16. DBWE 11:377–78.
17. DBWE 14:167, 169.

CHAPTER FIVE

The Beginning Church Struggle, 1933

Hitler Takes Power

Nationalist and National Socialist sentiments had been growing throughout Germany since the 1920s, particularly after the Great Depression in 1929 and the resulting high unemployment. These were supported by the sense of injustice most Germans felt at the reparations that had been demanded by the Versailles Treaty. Germans saw potential for a new German future in national consolidation, and the governmental crises of the Weimar Republic nourished skepticism in democracy. In the 1930 parliamentary elections the National Socialist Party (NSDAP) received 18.3 percent of the votes; in the July and November 1932 elections it reached 37.4 and 33.1 percent, becoming the strongest force in the parliament. Reich President Paul von Hindenburg named Adolf Hitler Reich Chancellor on January 30, 1933.

The Bonhoeffer family saw the dangers lurking in the person of Adolf Hitler. Dietrich Bonhoeffer's father, Karl, wrote later in his memoirs:

> From the start, we regarded the victory of National Socialism in 1933 and Hitler's appointment as Reich Chancellor as a misfortune—the entire family agreed on this. In my own case, I disliked and mistrusted

Hitler because of his demagogic propagandistic speeches, his telegram of condolence after the Potempa murder [in 1932, S.A. members in the Silesian village of Potempa beat a young Communist to death in front of his mother], his habit of driving about the country carrying a riding crop, his choice of colleagues . . . and finally because of what I heard from professional colleagues about his psychopathic symptoms.[1]

Dietrich Bonhoeffer analyzed these developments in a radio lecture that had been long planned on "The Führer and the Individual in the Younger Generation"; it was broadcast only two days after Hitler took power and was cut off because Bonhoeffer ran over his allotted time. Bonhoeffer spoke pointedly about Hitler's seductive potential without naming him:

> People and especially youth will feel the need to give a leader authority over them as long as they do not feel themselves to be mature, strong, responsible enough to themselves fulfill the demands placed in this authority. The leader will have to be responsibly aware of this clear restriction of authority. . . . if the leader tries to become the idol the led are looking for—something the led always hope from their leader—then the image of the leader shifts to one of a misleader.[2]

The Situation of the Church

Hitler tried to win over the churches through his skillful use of Christian and religious language, and he tried in other ways to give the impression that ultimately they were fighting for the same cause and that the churches would have some influence in the new system. Many church leaders succumbed to this tempting perspective. At the same time the National Socialists began pursuing their own aims. On February 28, 1933, the day after the Reichstag burned, Hitler decreed a state of emergency, allowing extensive curbs on civil liberties. The Enabling Act of March 24 gave him unlimited legislative powers. On April 1, 1933, the National Socialists called for the boycott of Jewish businesses, and on April 7 they passed the "Law for the Restoration of the Civil

---

1. Eberhard Bethge, *Dietrich Bonhoeffer: A Biography*, trans. Eric Mosbacher, et al., rev. and ed. Victoria J. Barnett (Minneapolis: Fortress Press, 2000), 258.
2. DBWE 12:280.

Service," with the so-called Aryan paragraph: all civil servants with a Jewish parent or grandparent had to be retired or dismissed from state employment.

There was a sector in the Protestant Church that identified itself theologically and politically with the Nazi cause. Founded in 1932, the German Christian Faith Movement (*Glaubensbewegung Deutsche Christen*) sought to bring National Socialism into the church. In the words of their June 6, 1932, guidelines:

> We wish to emphasize the reawakened German vitality of our church and revive our church. In the fatal struggle for the German freedom and future the church leadership has shown itself to be too weak. . . . We want our church to fight at the head of the decisive struggle for the existence or nonexistence of our people. . . . In race, ethnicity and nation we see orders of life given and bestowed upon us by God, and it is God's law that we tend to their preservation. . . . We know something about Christian duty and love toward the helpless, but we also demand that our people be protected from the incapable and less worthy. . . . We view the mission to the Jews as a serious threat to our ethnonational traditions (*Volkstum*). It is the doorway of alien blood into our national body. . . . In particular, marriage between Germans and Jews should be forbidden. . . .[3]

The desire spread quickly for a unified church, regulated by the "Führer principle." But it was the Aryan paragraph that triggered the debate within the German Protestant churches that became the Church Struggle (*Kirchenkampf*). Implementation of the April 1st state law within the churches was left up to the churches, and the German Christians immediately began to push for such regulations throughout the German regional churches. During the spring and summer of 1933 theologians and church leaders alike began to debate the issue, and the July 1933 national church elections, in which the German Christians gained control of most regional churches, led to the adoption of the Aryan paragraph for clergy and religious educators in many parts of Germany.

This issue directly affected Bonhoeffer because of his circle of friends. His friend and fellow pastor Franz Hildebrandt had a Jewish mother. In addition, Bonhoeffer's brother-in-law Gerhard Leibholz (who was married to

---

3. From Heiko A. Oberman, et al., eds., *Kirchen- und Theologiegeschichte in Quellen* IV/2 (Neukirchen-Vluyn: Neukirchener Verlag, 1980), 118f.

Bonhoeffer's twin sister Sabine) came from a Jewish family; Leibholz would emigrate in 1938 with his wife and daughters to London. Bonhoeffer viewed the introduction of an Aryan paragraph into church law as something that would fundamentally disrupt the nature of the church, since the criteria for church law differed from that of the state. He reacted by writing "The Church and the Jewish Question," which was published in June 1933. The first section of the essay, which addresses the church's task in light of the special state laws affecting Jews, takes up certain elements of the Lutheran understanding of authority. This was based on the distinct, divinely given tasks of state and church, which meant that the church was not to interfere with the state's political decisions. Bonhoeffer argues analogously:

> There is no doubt that the church of the Reformation is not encouraged to get involved directly in specific political actions of the state. The church has neither to praise nor to censure the laws of the state. Instead, it has to affirm the state as God's order of preservation in this godless world. It should recognize and understand the state's creation of order—whether good or bad from a humanitarian perspective—as grounded in God's desire for preservation in the midst of the world's chaotic godlessness. . . . The actions of the state remain free from interference by the church. . . . History is made not by the church but rather by the state.[4]

The "Jewish question" was "one of the historical problems that must be dealt with by our state . . . and without doubt the state is entitled to strike new paths in doing so."[5] For that reason, it was not the church's task to criticize the state in its dealings with Jews from the viewpoint of some kind of "humanitarian ideal." "Even on the Jewish question today, the church cannot contradict the state *directly* and demand that it take any particular different course of action."[6] But it could and should—and with this demand Bonhoeffer was criticizing the Lutheran concept of authority of his times—ask the state if it was fulfilling its duty and responsibility justly. The church had to ask the state whether its actions were actions that corresponded to its duty to realize and preserve justice and order. And this was precisely what the church in that moment had to do with respect to the Jewish question.

---

4. DBWE 12:362–63.
5. DBWE 12:363.
6. DBWE 12:363.

Bonhoeffer also wrote that the church had the task of helping the victims of the state's actions, that is, to become active in a charitable sense, entirely independent of whether the victims were church members or not. This, too, was what the situation demanded.

Bonhoeffer's wording for the third possibility of church action toward the state has become well known:

> The *third* possibility is not just to bind up the wounds of the victims beneath the wheel but to seize the wheel itself. Such an action would be direct political action on the part of the church. This is only possible and called for if the church sees the state to be failing in its function of creating law and order, that is, if the church perceives that the state, without any restraints, has created either too much or too little law and order.[7]

This third kind of church action would become necessary if a group of subjects of the state lose their rights or if the state interfered with the nature of the church through excluding baptized Jews from the church or banning the missions to the Jews. What does this third option mean when it refers to "seizing the wheel itself"? This text has repeatedly been interpreted to mean that Bonhoeffer was already thinking of violent resistance in 1933 with his use of this drastic, combative image. In recent years, however, doubts have grown about this interpretation. In the text itself Bonhoeffer writes that the church would then be in *status confessionis*, that is, in a confessional situation in which for the sake of the confession to Christ there was only one position that is in accordance with the confession to Christ.

From Bonhoeffer's perspective this situation began a short time later. In the July 23, 1933, church elections the German Christians attained a majority in most regional churches. In September 1933, through the resolution of the so-called Brown Synod (many church delegates appeared in brown NSDAP uniforms), the Aryan paragraph was implemented in the Church of the Old Prussian Union, to which Bonhoeffer belonged. This negated the sole valid criterion for the office of ministry in the Protestant Church, which had been established in the Reformation and was valid for the Old Prussian Union Church as well: the pastor must only be *rite vocatus*, that is, properly called to the ministry by the church. Enraged, Bonhoeffer wrote Karl Barth:

---

7. DBWE 12:365–66.

You have written [in your text *Theological Existence Today!*] that wherever a church introduces the Aryan paragraph, it ceases to be a Christian church. . . . Now that which was to be expected has happened, and I therefore ask you in the name of many friends, pastors, and students, please to let us know whether you consider it possible to stay in a church that has ceased to be a Christian church, that is, whether one may continue to exercise within it the office of pastor when that office has become a privilege for Aryans. . . . Several of us are now very drawn to the idea of a free church. . . . There can be no doubt that a *status confessionis* exists, but what is the most appropriate way today to express what the *confessio* says?—that is not clear to us. . . .[8]

Barth agreed that this was a *status confessionis*, and encouraged Bonhoeffer to make it clear to the church government that, with the incorporation of the Aryan paragraph, "In this respect, you are no longer the church of Christ!"[9] Yet he advised a "highly active, polemical position of waiting";[10] leaving the church could only be the *ultima ratio*. Bonhoeffer's letter to Barth makes clear that the *status confessionis* had not occurred through the Aryan paragraph as such but through the implementation of this state law in the realm of the church, for it challenged the very nature of the church, which should not make the access to Christ dependent on external laws.

On September 11, 1933, Martin Niemöller, Dietrich Bonhoeffer, and others founded the Pastors Emergency League, an organization intended to assist the pastors who could no longer support themselves due to the implementation of the Aryan paragraph and to attack the views of the German Christians through different forms of publicity. The Pastors Emergency League submitted a protest statement to the national synod in Wittenberg on September 27, which Bonhoeffer signed and which charged that the church had been "turned into a kingdom of this world by the rule of force and the denial of fraternal love."[11] The Aryan paragraph, it stated, contradicted the Bible and confession, and it limited the gospel through human laws. A few months later the Confessing Church would emerge from the Pastors Emergency League.

---

8. DBWE 12:164–65.
9. DBWE 12:167.
10. DBWE 12:168.
11. DBWE 12:182.

In the summer of 1933 Bonhoeffer had already been part of a group under the leadership of Friedrich von Bodelschwingh that was working on a confession in light of the church situation. He refused to sign the final version of this document, the Bethel Confession, published at the end of 1933, because in his view it had been watered down. The August 1933 version that he supported unequivocally criticized the "natural theology" that expected God's revelation in the creation and in history, beyond Christ's revelation:

> We reject the false doctrine that in a particular "hour of history" God is speaking to us directly and is revealed in direct action in the created world, for it is Enthusiasm to think that one understands the will of God without the express words of the Holy Scriptures, to which God is bound. ("God said, 'Let there be the people [*Volk*]!' and there was the people."—Hossenfelder [Reich leader of the German Christians])[12]

Accordingly, this text criticized—as did Bonhoeffer's book *Creation and Fall*—the German Christians' theological concept of "orders of life" or "of creation." This was the assumption that there are certain orders in this world God firmly established in the creation and which human beings have to follow—for example, that a man and woman should enter into marriage with one another, or that people of the same race belong to one people and that the people (*Volk*) had the duty to fight for the existence of their own. Such sentiments were expressed by Wilhelm Stählin, a professor of practical theology:

> As long as the peoples threaten or violate each other in the necessary space for life (*Lebensraum*) and the unfolding of what they are determined to do, struggle for the life and freedom of one's own people is one of the duties that binds us in our earthly situation; membership in the Christian church does not suspend these obligations, on the contrary it directs us to the earthly place where we are to prove obedience and faith.[13]

While Bonhoeffer in Barcelona had formulated something similar, now he was critical of this concept, stating that there was no order of creation valuable

---

12. DBWE 12:386.
13. Wilhelm Stählin, "Die Einheit der christlichen Kirche und die Völker," *Die Eiche* 20 (1932): 333.

for its own sake and good as such. There were only "orders of preservation," which had value because they preserved the world "for the sake of its future in Christ and the new creation."[14] Ultimately, the issue was that the world had to remain open for Christ. Wherever this did not occur, wherever there was no longer room for the proclamation of the gospel, then it was no longer an order of God and—as in the case of the allegiance to the concept of the Volk—had to be abandoned. Bonhoeffer had already made a similar argument in his book *Creation and Fall*: the orders given by God in this world "are God's orders of preservation that uphold and preserve us for Christ. They are not orders of creation but orders of preservation. They have no value in themselves; instead they find their end and meaning only through Christ."[15]

Given the turbulent political and church situation, it may seem odd at first glance that Bonhoeffer in the summer of 1933 held his lectures at University of Berlin only about Christology, the church teachings about Jesus Christ. In this lecture Bonhoeffer unpacked one of his core theological concepts: Christology does not mean imagining a good human being that one should take as a model, nor is it a matter of some interesting historical theological quibbles. In facing Jesus Christ it is "the question of faith: Who are you? Are you God's very self?,"[16] as well as answering the question that comes back at us: "Who are you, that you ask this question?"[17] One could not deal with Jesus Christ at an academic distance but, rather, in Bonhoeffer's opinion, through opening oneself to encountering this person. Jesus Christ alone has the authority to ask these questions of human beings and thus to claim the human *for himself*. Other human beings have authority only because another has given it to them—and the political dimension of this statement cannot be overlooked. As a whole, the lecture leaves no doubt that the church is to orient itself toward Christ—and nothing else. It was a radical stand that ran in direct opposition to the growing church support for National Socialism.

For Bonhoeffer's path, the changes in his church in 1933 had far-reaching consequences: in September he decided to take a pastorate in a German overseas congregation in London, beginning in October. He wrote Karl Barth shortly after his arrival in London:

---

14. DBWE 12:387.
15. DBWE 3:140.
16. DBWE 12:302.
17. DBWE 12:305.

. . . I also received an offer of a pastorate in east Berlin and was certain of the vote there. Then came the Aryan paragraph in the Prussian church, and I knew that I could not accept that pastorate for which I had been longing, particularly in that part of the city, if I was unwilling to give up my unconditional opposition to *this* church. It would have meant the loss of credibility before the congregation from the outset. It would have meant abandoning my solidarity with the Jewish Christian pastors—my closest friend (Franz Hildebrandt) is one of them and is currently without a future, so he is now coming to join me in England. . . . If it is at all desirable, after such a decision, to find well-defined reasons for it, I think one of the strongest was that I no longer felt inwardly equal to the questions and demands that I was facing. I felt that, in some way I don't understand, I found myself in radical opposition to all my friends; I was becoming increasingly isolated with my views of the matter. . . . All this frightened me and shook my confidence, so that I began to fear that dogmatism might be leading me astray. . . . And so I thought it was about time to go into the wilderness for a spell, and simply work as a pastor, as unobtrusively as possible.[18]

18. DBWE 13:22–23.

CHAPTER SIX

PASTOR IN LONDON, 1933–1935

The "Calm of the Parish Ministry"

Bonhoeffer took up his duties in London on October 17, 1933. He was responsible for the German Reformed congregation of St. Paul's in Whitechapel and the German Evangelical[1] congregation in Sydenham-Forest Hill. Before leaving Berlin he had been summoned before the church leadership to justify various critical statements he had made about recent church developments and was told that he couldn't be allowed to go abroad with such positions. Bonhoeffer did not allow this to bother him, however; he told Reich Bishop Ludwig Müller "that under no circumstances could I represent the German Christians, that I would continue to express my position in ecumenical conversations, and that if he expected anything different from me, I would prefer that he forbid me to go."[2] Not all his friends and allies understood how Bonhoeffer could withdraw from the immediate church controversies in Germany. Karl Barth,

---

1. Throughout this book, "German Evangelical Church" is used to refer to the Protestant Church in Germany.
2. DBWE 13:30.

who was intensively involved in these from his position in Bonn, responded indignantly to Bonhoeffer's letter from London:

> . . . now that you have come to me with this after the fact, I truly cannot do otherwise than call to you, "Get back to your post in Berlin straight-away!" What is this about "going into the wilderness," "the calm of the parish ministry," and so forth at a moment when you are needed in Ger-many? You, who know as well as I do that . . . [u]nder no circumstances should you now be playing Elijah under the juniper tree or Jonah under the gourd; you need to be here with all guns blazing! What's the point of singing my praises—from the other side of the Channel? . . . [you must] think only of one thing: that you are a German, that your church's house is on fire, that you know enough, and know well enough how to say what you know, to be able to help, and in fact you ought to return to your post by the next ship! Well, let's say, with the one after that.[3]

For the time being, however, Bonhoeffer did not let this distract him. He began to assist German refugees, introduced children's Sunday school in the Sydenham church, and in both congregations set up special youth programs. Meanwhile, very few adult parishioners attended Sunday worship. Bonhoeffer preached in a direct, unvarnished tone that was hardly an invitation to con-templative edification:

> We do believe in all sorts of things, far too many things in fact. We believe in power, we believe in ourselves and in other people, we believe in humankind. We believe in our own people [Volk] and in our reli-gious community, we believe in new ideas—but in the midst of all those things, we do not believe in the One—in God. And believing in God would take away our faith in all the other powers, make it impossible to believe in them. If you believe in God, you don't believe in anything else in this world, because you know it will all break down and pass away.[4]

---

3. DBWE 13:39–41; trans. altered.
4. DBWE 13:405–6.

"The Disloyal Clergy Abroad"

From London Bonhoeffer continued to follow the political and church developments in Germany. On November 13, 1933, the leader of the Berlin German Christians, Reinhold Krause, publicly called for an ethnic church at the Sport Palace rally of the German Christians. The church, he declared, had to liberate itself "from the Old Testament with its Jewish economic morality, from these tales of cattle traders and pimps," and reject "the entire scapegoat and inferior theology of Rabbi Paul": "When we draw from the gospel that which speaks to our German hearts," Krause concluded, "then the essentials of the teaching of Jesus emerge clearly and revealingly, coinciding completely with the demands of National Socialism, and we can be proud of that."[5] Members of the Pastors Emergency League—as well as many moderate members of the German Christians—were outraged by the failure of the church leaders who attended to protest these plans to alter the Bible and their adoption in the meeting's closing resolution. In the widespread uproar that followed, the heads of the Pastors Emergency League managed to pressure the Reich bishop to suspend Krause temporarily. Joachim Hossenfelder, a German Christian leader who had been bishop of Brandenburg since September 1933, resigned his post shortly thereafter. The application of the Aryan paragraph in the Prussian church was blocked for the time being.

The Sport Palace debacle put wind into the sails of the church opposition to the German Christians, and the opposition now hoped that things had reached a turning point. Bonhoeffer was demanding a church trial on doctrine that could finally establish the heresy of German Christian theology. Again and again he tried from London to influence developments in Germany. Almost all the German pastors serving in England became involved in the German developments by sending opinions and telegrams to the Reich church leadership in Berlin and the church opposition. In January 1934 they threatened that their parishes would break from the German Evangelical Church and demanded the resignation of Reich Bishop Ludwig Müller. The German church leadership in Berlin was quite unhappy about such disruptions. Bishop Theodor Heckel, whose office in Berlin oversaw all the overseas congregations, wrote a letter to all the overseas pastors in January 1934:

---

5. Klaus Scholder, *The Churches and the Third Reich*, vol. 1: *Preliminary History and the Time of Illusions*, trans. John Bowden (Philadelphia: Fortress Press, 1988), 553; trans. altered.

In particular I must urgently impress upon the clergy abroad the necessity for the greatest possible discretion in regard to church politics. Just as the soldier at the front is not in a position to assess the overall plan but must carry out the duties that immediately concern him, so I expect the clergy abroad to distinguish between their own particular task and the task of the church authorities in shaping the German Evangelical Church at home.[6]

In February Heckel made a visit to the London congregations to convince the pastors—unsuccessfully—to abandon their disloyalty to the Reich bishop.

Bonhoeffer openly discussed the developments in Germany with the leading personalities of the ecumenical movement. His most important contact was Bishop George Bell, the Anglican bishop of Chichester who was president of the ecumenical Council for Life and Work. Bell and Bonhoeffer had met during the 1932 ecumenical meeting in Geneva. Bonhoeffer felt that ecumenical support for the church opposition was indispensable, particularly in view of a possible and politically delicate institutional break by the church opposition from the Reich church. On April 15, 1934, he wrote Bell: ". . . the moment has definitely come for the ecumenic movement either to take a definite attitude—perhaps in the way of an ultimatum or in expressing publicly the sympathy with the oppositional pastors—or to loose all confidence among the best element of the german pastors. . . ."[7] In consultation with Bonhoeffer Bell wrote letters and position papers to German leaders and institutions to make the ecumenical position clear. Heckel also visited Bell in February 1934 in an unsuccessful attempt to move him to refrain from such intervention.

The synod of the German Evangelical Church in Wuppertal-Barmen, from May 29 to May 31, 1934, proved to be decisive for the months that followed. On April 22 a meeting of church opposition leaders in Ulm had declared that they represented the true church in Germany, and on May 29 the first confessional synod of the Prussian churches laid the groundwork for what would become the Confessing Church. This was followed on May 30–31 by a national synod of German church leaders, attended by 139 representatives from the twenty-six regional churches. Impelled by their opposition to the extremism of the German Christians, these delegates unanimously approved the Barmen Theological Declaration.

---

6. DBWE 13:91–92.
7. DBWE 13:128; the prose reflects Bonhoeffer's original English.

The renowned Barmen Theological Declaration, written mostly by Karl Barth, consists of six theses, each beginning with one or two biblical citations followed by a short affirmative doctrinal statement and one or two condemnations of the German Christians' distortion of these teachings. The goal was to undergird the foundation of Protestant faith "in light of the heresies of the German Christians which have devastated the church and destroyed the unity of the German Evangelical Church" and to combat "the alien presuppositions" that had been introduced by the German Christians and through which the church ceased "to be church."[8] Bonhoeffer welcomed the founding of the Confessing Church and the Theological Declaration. Its first thesis emphasized what he himself viewed as decisive in this crisis:

> Jesus Christ, as he is attested to us in Holy Scripture, is the one Word of God which we have to hear, and which we have to trust and obey in life and in death.

> We reject the false doctrine that the church could and should recognize as a source of its proclamation, beyond and besides this one Word of God, yet other events, powers, historic figures, and truths as God's revelation.[9]

Bonhoeffer's Peace Speech in Fanø

In the summer of 1934 it was not just the church situation that was tense; the international political situation was also becoming more strained. Germany had left the League of Nations on October 14, 1933. Bonhoeffer believed that international church encounters were all the more important. After the clear repudiation of the teachings of the German Christians in Barmen, he found it unthinkable to meet with them at ecumenical meetings. In August 1934 the World Alliance and the Ecumenical Council for Life and Work planned to hold a joint conference in Fanø, Denmark. In advance Bonhoeffer made it clear, on behalf of Martin Niemöller and Karl Koch, the president of the Confessing synod, that the ecumenical councils needed to extend an official

---

8. From Alfred Burgsmüller and Rudolf Weth, eds., *Die Barmer Theologische Erklärung. Einführung und Dokumentation*, 6th ed. (Neukirchen-Vluyn: Neukirchener Verlag, 1998), 34ff.
9. Cited from Matthew Hockenos, *A Church Divided: German Protestants Confront the Nazi Past* (Bloomington: Indiana University Press, 2004), 179.

Dietrich Bonhoeffer with Jean Lasserre at the ecumenical meeting in Fanø, 1934

invitation to a representative of the Confessing Church as a sign of recognizing the Barmen synod. With that, the Confessing Church hoped to be recognized as representing the legitimate German Evangelical Church. After extensive negotiations two representatives of the Confessing synod were invited as guests. At the same time Bonhoeffer demanded that the conference pass a resolution that would make clear "that we are immediately faced with the decision: National Socialist *or* Christian."[10] Indeed, a collective ecumenical resolution was passed in Fanø that clearly criticized the church policies of the German government and ensured prayers and sympathy for the Confessing Church. Bonhoeffer and Karl Koch (who did not attend) were elected "consultative and co-opted members" of the Council on Life and Work. The Confessing Church viewed it as an important signal. Bonhoeffer thanked Bell: "I

---

10. DBWE 13:192.

want to thank you very much for the great help you have rendered to the cause of our Church at the Fanø Conference. The resolution in its final form has become a true expression of a brotherly spirit, of justice and truthfulness."[11] At the same time, however, the resolution included the sentence that the ecumenical movement wanted to maintain friendly relations with all sectors of the German Evangelical Church, including the German Christians, thereby falling short of an unequivocal position.

In Fanø Bonhoeffer also held a talk on "The Church and the Peoples of the World." As he had already done in 1932, he urgently emphasized the special significance of the ecumenical dimension of the church for the world. While the Christian church always existed in a specific national and political context, he noted, at the same time it transcended this context. Because the ecumenical movement had taken up God's summons for peace, it needed now to direct this toward the peoples of the world, irrespective of national ties and interests. For Bonhoeffer, to question this summons was to pose the question of the serpent in Genesis 3:

> "Has God not understood human nature well enough to know that wars must occur in this world, like laws of nature? Must God not have meant that we should talk about peace, to be sure, but that it is not to be literally translated into action? Must God not really have said that we should work for peace, of course, but also make ready tanks and poison gas for security?" And then perhaps the most serious question: "Did God say you should not protect your own people? Did God say you should leave your own a prey to the enemy?" No, God did not say all that. What He has said is that there shall be peace among men—that we shall obey Him without further question, that is what He means. He who questions the commandment of God before obeying has already denied Him.[12]

Instead, the ecumenical movement needed to remind the world: "Brothers . . . cannot take up arms against Christ himself—yet this is what they do if they take up arms against one another."[13] Bonhoeffer soberly observed that peace could not be reached by taking the path of security. Whoever wanted security would necessarily be distrustful of the other, and precisely this was what

---

11. DBWE 13:213–14; the prose reflects Bonhoeffer's original English.
12. DBWE 13:307–8.
13. DBWE 13:308.

supported war. In contrast, peace was always a risk, a dare in which one yields completely to God's command. The task of the church gathered in Fanø was to proclaim this command:

> Who will call us to peace so that the world will hear, will have to hear? . . . Only the one great Ecumenical Council of the Holy Church of Christ over all the world can speak out so that the world, though it gnash its teeth, will have to hear, so that the peoples will rejoice because the Church of Christ in the name of Christ has taken the weapons from the hands of their sons, forbidden war, and proclaimed the peace of Christ against the raging world. . . . The Ecumenical Council is in session. . . . The hour is late. The world is choked with weapons, and dreadful is the distrust which looks out of all men's eyes. The trumpets of war may blow tomorrow. For what are we waiting?[14]

In the months that followed the Confessing Church continued to take shape in Germany. The second Confessing synod in Dahlem on October 19–20, 1934, declared a state of emergency in the church and established distinct church governing bodies to oversee Confessing congregations. Bonhoeffer's congregations in London joined the Confessing Church, as did almost all the German parishes in England.

Return to Germany

In London Dietrich Bonhoeffer continued to ponder the appropriate form for the church opposition to take. He wrote his Swiss friend Erwin Sutz in April 1934:

> And while I'm working with the church opposition with all my might, it's perfectly clear to me that *this* opposition is only a very temporary transitional phase on the way to an opposition of a very different kind, and that very few of those involved in this preliminary skirmish are going to be there for that second struggle. I believe that all of Christendom should be praying with us for the coming of resistance "to the point of shedding blood" and for the finding of people who can suffer it through. Simply suffering is what it will be about, not parries, blows,

---

14. DBWE 13:309.

or thrusts such as may still be allowed and possible in the preliminary battles; the real struggle that perhaps lies ahead must be one of simply suffering through in faith. Then, perhaps then God will acknowledge his church again with his word, but until then a great deal must be believed, and prayed, and suffered.[15]

At first glance, it seems as if Bonhoeffer in this letter is already willing to suffer the consequences of participating in the violent overthrow of Hitler. Closer observation, however, shows that he was thinking of a passive, silent resistance, one that emphasized not the shifting of worldly powers, but God's standing by his church anew. Bonhoeffer hoped for this as a consequence of the steadfast orientation around Jesus' Sermon on the Mount:

> You know, it is my belief—perhaps it will amaze you—that it is the *Sermon on the Mount* that has the deciding word on this whole affair. . . . Please write and tell me sometime how you preach about the Sermon on the Mount. I'm currently trying to do so, to keep it infinitely plain and simple, but it always comes back to *keeping* the commandments and not trying to evade them. *Following* Christ—what that really is, I'd like to know—it is not exhausted by our concept of faith. I'm doing some writing that I think of as a "spiritual exercise"—only as a first step. . . . How long I shall remain a pastor, and how long in this church, I don't know. Possibly not very long. This winter I'd like to go to India.[16]

Bonhoeffer did not travel to India, where he wanted to meet Mahatma Gandhi and learn about the methods of nonviolent resistance. But in March 1935 he visited a number of Christian communities and seminaries to collect impressions of other forms of church life that could overcome National Socialism from within:

> I think I am right in saying that I would only achieve true inner clarity and honesty by really starting to take the Sermon on the Mount seriously. Here alone lies the force that can blow all this hocus-pocus sky-high—like fireworks, leaving only a few burnt-out shells behind. The restoration of the church must surely depend on a new kind of

---

15. DBWE 13:135.
16. DBWE 13:135–36.

monasticism, which has nothing in common with the old but a life of uncompromising discipleship, following Christ according to the Sermon on the Mount. I believe the time has come to gather people together and do this. . . . Things do exist that are worth standing up for without compromise. To me it seems that peace and social justice are such things, as is Christ himself.[17]

With these convictions Bonhoeffer returned to Germany in April 1935, at the request of the Confessing Church Council of Brethren, to direct a newly founded preachers' seminary for the Confessing Church.

---

17. DBWE 13:284–85.

CHAPTER SEVEN

DIRECTOR OF A PREACHERS' SEMINARY, 1935–1937

Brotherly Life

One consequence of the emergency law declared by the Dahlem synod was the decision by the Old Prussian Union Church to oversee the theological training of its pastors. In addition to two church colleges in Wuppertal-Elberfeld and Berlin (both of which were immediately banned by the police, but continued to operate illegally), five independent preachers' seminaries were founded: in Elberfeld and Bielefeld, in the eastern Prussian town of Bloestau, in Naumburg, and in Pomerania. Many of the candidates—young men[1] who were serving as vicars in the Confessing Church—had already been in prison because of their loyalty to the Confessing Church. The training in the preachers' seminary was intended to give them time to reflect theologically

---

1. Translator's note: The first generation of German women to study theology started their careers just as the Church Struggle was beginning, and many of them became active in the Confessing Church, where they fought for the right to ordination. Because church law still barred them from full ordination to the ministry they were not allowed to study in the preachers' seminaries; nonetheless, many of them served as vicars (and some were eventually ordained as exceptions after the war began and most male clergy were drafted into military service).

Dietrich Bonhoeffer in August 1935

on their practical experience; after that they would be ordained. After the Fifth Implementation Decree of the Law to Restore Order in the German Evangelical Church was decreed at the end of 1935, these newly ordained clergy could only be placed as assistants under a Confessing Church pastor or in a patronage parish, that is, a parish on an estate in which the owner of the estate (landed nobility) could select the pastor. Those who chose to attend a preachers' seminary of the Confessing Church were relinquishing a secure position in the Reich church.

Bonhoeffer became director of studies for the preachers' seminary in Pomerania. His first session began in April 1935 in the Zingsthof, a retreat center of the Westphalian church's student Bible circle that was located on the Baltic peninsula of Zingst. Wilhelm Rott, a Reformed pastor from Rhineland, joined him as inspector of studies. There were around twenty to twenty-five candidates who attended these sessions, each of which lasted about six months. The first session was attended by Eberhard Bethge, who later became Bonhoeffer's biographer and director of the Rhineland church's pastoral college from 1962 to 1976, and Albrecht Schönherr, who later became bishop of Berlin-Brandenburg in the German Democratic Republic and chaired the Protestant Church Federation there. Gerhard Ebeling, later one of the most significant twentieth-century German Luther and dogmatics scholars, participated in the fourth session.

After the vacation season began in mid-June 1935, the Zingst retreat center was no longer available, and the group moved to Finkenwalde, a former estate near the town of Stettin. The house had almost no furniture and the candidates wrote a poetic appeal to potential donors. Several congregations and individuals responded generously by donating furniture, books, and other gifts, and continued to support the work there through their prayers and monetary gifts. In return, the members of the Finkenwalde community served the Confessing Church parishes in Finkenwalde and Stettin. They also began so-called evangelization mission trips (*Volksmissionsfahrten*) to different parishes throughout the region, where they held worship services and offered children's classes. Eberhard Bethge described these mission trips in one of the Finkenwalde circular letters:

> . . . it was a self-evident part of this work that every morning the brothers held devotions, a short period of silence before the worship service and then devotions in the church after the service. We learned again how wonderful it is not to have to stand alone in our proclamation; the community supports every word, also through their prayers, and if someone failed, another would jump in.[2]

The preachers' seminary was especially supported by Ruth von Kleist-Retzow, who lived on an estate in Klein-Krössin near Kieckow. Her grandchildren had moved in with her and were attending a secondary school in Stettin after the private schools they attended fell under National Socialist influence. Bonhoeffer and the older woman developed an intense exchange about theological, church, and political questions, and he became a regular guest on her estate. Her granddaughters—Maria von Wedemeyer and Ruth-Alice von Wedemeyer, who was already engaged at the time to Klaus von Bismarck—occasionally visited the worship services in Finkenwalde.

Bonhoeffer believed that the preachers' seminary should not be a fellowship for its own sake, but that it needed to prepare its seminarians for the Church Struggle: "The goal is not monastic isolation but rather the most

---

2. Ilse Tödt, ed., *Die Finkenwalder Rundbriefe. Briefe und Texte von Dietrich Bonhoeffer und seinen Predigerseminaristen 1935–1946* (Gütersloh: Gütersloher Verlagshaus, 2013), 160.

intensive concentration for ministry to the world."[3] Only this could overcome the "isolation" of the parish ministry and the "burden of proclamation." Only a "proclamation that derives from a community that is lived and experienced in a more practical fashion will, in its own turn, be more objective and imperturbable and will be less likely to run aground."[4] Through a life in fellowship that followed God's commandments, "a strict Christian life in prayer, meditation, scriptural reflection, and discussions with his brothers," the church's proclamation might become credible once again.[5]

With the beginning of the second session a House of Brethren was formed to support the seminary's work. It consisted of a group of unmarried men who could concentrate fully on mentoring the candidates and maintaining contact with former seminarians. They also organized retreats for former seminarians. Eberhard Bethge and Fritz Onnasch became permanent members of the House of Brethren, and in the fifth session Onnasch succeeded Wilhelm Rott as inspector of studies.

The House of Brethren also sent monthly circular letters, which became the most important form of contact with former seminarians. These circular letters reported on the parish work of former seminarians, but also posted news of those who had been imprisoned for their opposition to the Nazi regime, were soldiers on the front, or had died in the war. The circular letters called them all to prayer for each other, reported on the current activities in the preachers' seminary, and encouraged the former seminarians to hold fast to what they had learned. The letters included sermon meditations that helped them continue to work together on sermons despite being in different places. In addition, they included positions on current issues and lists of the biblical texts being used for the morning devotions in Finkenwalde, so that all the brothers, current and former, could remain connected through a common biblical reflection.

Daily life in the preachers' seminary followed a strict schedule. The core of theological courses consisted of lectures on the New Testament that eventually formed Bonhoeffer's 1937 book *Nachfolge* [ET: *Discipleship*], as well as lectures on practical theology. The latter included lectures on preaching, catechetical classes (for children and youth), and pastoral care. But the students

---

3. DBWE 14:96.
4. DBWE 14:95.
5. DBWE 14:96.

also studied the Old Testament, central issues in the church constitution, the confessional writings from the Reformation, and dogmatics.

In addition to theological training, common spiritual life was central. Times were set for common devotions in the mornings and evenings; these included scriptural meditation as well as group hymn singing. Bethge reported that Bonhoeffer's rule that each candidate had to meditate for a half hour every morning proved to be especially difficult for them. In one of the discussions about this,

> . . . some people said they went to sleep, others that they spent the half hour working on sermons, since they had absolutely no idea what else to do; others admitted that half an hour's recollection was too much for them and their minds wandered, so they read commentaries instead. . . . Other seminaries were already regarding Zingst as a joke—a place, they said, where the ordinands had to meditate while they brushed their teeth. . . .[6]

Bonhoeffer didn't drop the rule, but eased it somewhat by scheduling a group meditation once a week. He also had the brothers take the opportunity regularly to confess to one another individually. There were a number of other principles that Bonhoeffer had created for their life together. Probably the most difficult one was that that no one should speak about another brother in his absence.

Bonhoeffer was quickly accused of having created a legalistic way of life in Finkenwalde, a charge he energetically refuted:

> The reproach that it is somehow legalistic does not really concern me. What is legalistic if a Christian should learn what it means to pray and spend a good portion of his time learning to do so? A leader in the Confessing Church recently told me that "we have no time now for meditation; candidates should learn how to preach and how to conduct catechism classes"; this statement attests either a total lack of knowledge of what young theologians actually are today or a blasphemous lack of knowledge with respect to how a sermon and catechesis come about. The questions young theologians are seriously asking us today are: How can I

---

6. Eberhard Bethge, *Dietrich Bonhoeffer: A Biography*, trans. Eric Mosbacher, et al., rev. and ed. Victoria J. Barnett (Minneapolis: Fortress Press, 2000), 463.

learn to pray? How can I learn to read Scripture? If we do not help them with these questions, we are not helping them at all.[7]

Many of the candidates who studied in Finkenwalde later described it as one of the most influential periods of their lives. Bonhoeffer himself wrote the participants at the end of the first session: "The summer of 1935 was, I believe, the most fulfilling period in my entire life thus far both professionally and personally . . . by living together with all of you I learned more than ever in both respects."[8]

Discipleship

After his time in New York, and particularly during the period in London, Bonhoeffer had been thinking about the Sermon on the Mount and its consequences for those who wished to shape their lives according to it. For him, the Sermon on the Mount was not a list of ethical principles (such as always loving one's enemies) but the spelling out of what it means to follow Jesus Christ. This orientation toward discipleship to Jesus Christ became increasingly important to him during the Church Struggle, when a church that held itself back from political power was mocked. In that context, it was helpful to reflect on where, from a Christian perspective, one could find God:

> Where is your God? That is the question put to us, restlessly, despairingly, or derisively. Death, sin, distress and war, also bravery, power, and honor—such things one can see. But where is your God? No one need be ashamed of the tears one sheds over our not being able to see God, over not being able to prove God to our brothers. These tears are shed for God's sake and indeed are tears that God counts (Psalm 56:9). Where is your God? How else can we respond except to point to the man who in life, death, and resurrection proved to be God's true Son, Jesus Christ. In death, he is our life; in sin, our forgiveness; in distress, our helper; in war, our peace. "To this man you should point and say: that is God" (Luther).[9]

---

7. DBWE 14:254.
8. DBWE 14:119.
9. DBWE 14:848. Bonhoeffer here paraphrases Martin Luther, *The Babylonian Captivity of the Church*, in *Luther's Works*, vol. 36: *Word and Sacrament II*, ed. Helmut T. Lehman and Abdel R. Wentz (Philadelphia: Fortress Press, 1959), 35 [WA 6:511].

Through all five sessions at Finkenwalde Bonhoeffer addressed the theme of discipleship with different emphases. His final lecture at University of Berlin in the winter semester of 1935/36 had covered the same content. In explaining what discipleship meant he was at the same time describing what Christian life in the context of the Church Struggle had to look like. His Finkenwalde students hoped that he would create a book based on his lectures. As the March 1937 circular letter reported, for his birthday on February 4, 1937, the "wish . . . was this time reversed and the fourth session placed on its wish list: 1. 'Discipleship' should appear before we retire . . ."[10] The book was published at the end of 1937, becoming one of the most widely read Bonhoeffer books in the world.

The book opens with the warning not to be satisfied with "cheap grace":

Cheap grace is the mortal enemy of our church. Our struggle today is for costly grace. Cheap grace means grace as bargain-basement goods, cut-rate forgiveness, cut-rate comfort, cut-rate sacrament. . . . It is grace without a price, without costs. . . . Thus, the Christian should live the same way the world does. In all things the Christian should go along with the world and not venture to live a different life under grace from that under sin! . . . Cheap grace is that grace which we bestow on ourselves.[11]

For Christian life, however, the concern must be for costly grace:

Costly grace is the hidden treasure in the field, for the sake of which people go and sell with joy everything they have. It is the costly pearl, for whose price the merchant sells all that he has. . . . It is the call of Jesus Christ which causes a disciple to leave his nets and follow him. . . . It is costly, because it calls to discipleship; it is grace, because it calls us to follow *Jesus Christ*. It is costly, because it costs people their lives; it is grace, because it thereby makes them live. . . . Above all, grace is costly, because it was costly to God, because it costs God the life of God's Son and because nothing can be cheap to us which is costly to God.[12]

---

10. German editor's introduction to the German edition of *Nachfolge* [DBW 4], 12.
11. DBWE 4:43–44.
12. DBWE 4:44–45.

In speaking about costly grace Bonhoeffer was fighting a misunderstanding of Martin Luther's doctrine on justification, the center of which was the statement that God justifies human beings "through grace alone." This means that human beings must and can do nothing to be accepted by God. No good moral work, no religious deed can bring about God's acceptance. God accepts human beings without preconditions and solely out of grace. Human beings must only believe this and acknowledge it. According to Luther, only in this belief are human beings in a position to fulfill God's commandments without seeking their own advantage—that is, to be obedient. Bonhoeffer summed up Luther's teaching as follows: "only the believers obey."[13] According to Bonhoeffer, the misunderstanding stemmed from drawing the conclusion that God's grace demands no altered behavior or obedience. "Because grace alone does everything, everything can stay in its old ways,"[14] thereby separating faith from obedience. Bonhoeffer opposed this, pointing out that faith and obedience belong inherently together. Without obedience, without the human being living according to God's will, there is no faith. With that, discipleship is the situation in which both are true: *only the believers obey, and only the obedient believe.*"[15] It is an illusion to think that faith does not have to lead to a changed life.

With this foundation as the point of departure, Bonhoeffer then did an exegesis of different New Testament stories to show how Jesus called people as disciples. These stories speak of the obedience one must perform, of the suffering that discipleship means, and the isolation that comes through Jesus' call, illustrating the radicality of Christian discipleship:

> Those called leave everything they have . . . because otherwise they could not walk behind Jesus. . . . The disciple is thrown out of the relative security of life into complete insecurity (which in truth is absolute security and protection in community with Jesus); out of the foreseeable and calculable realm (which in truth is unreliable) into the completely unforeseeable, coincidental realm (which in truth is the only necessary and reliable one); out of the realm of limited possibilities (which in truth is that of unlimited possibilities) into the realm of unlimited possibilities (which in truth is the only liberating reality). Yet that is not a general law;

---

13. DBWE 4:63.
14. DBWE 4:43.
15. DBWE 4:63.

it is, rather, the exact opposite of all legalism. Again, it is nothing other than being bound to Jesus Christ alone.[16]

The core of the book is an interpretation of the Sermon on the Mount. Bonhoeffer describes the particular situation of the disciples as they led consequent lives of discipleship with Jesus and their liberation from worldly ties, and exhorts and encourages us to live this way. He makes no secret of the high price to be paid when one lives in discipleship, but he emphasizes repeatedly that this is worth the sacrifice, because the disciple is not alone—he or she has Christ as well as the wider fellowship of disciples.

In the second part of *Discipleship* Bonhoeffer discusses the problem that Jesus today does not encounter human beings as he did the apostles in his own time. Today, too, there is discipleship, but the call to discipleship and the life in discipleship are manifested differently, since they appear after the death, resurrection, and ascension of Jesus. The call to discipleship is manifested in the church, through the sermon and sacrament. It is the church—here Bonhoeffer repeats his earliest insights—in which Christ is present today. Today, baptism means no longer standing under the commitments of this world. Remaining in discipleship today is to remain in the church and the body of Christ. Bonhoeffer emphasizes that remaining in the church means staying in the visible church.

Viewed superficially, the book seems to proclaim a Christian spirituality that is alien to the world. Whoever looks more deeply, however, discovers clear political references—for example, in the reference (difficult for a reader today to follow) to "simple obedience" to Jesus' call, which Bonhoeffer describes as a contrast to the "blind obedience" demanded toward Hitler. In contrast to the dissolution of the individual person in the *Volk* community, Bonhoeffer determines that Jesus calls human beings as individuals to discipleship.

The concrete church political situation was also in the background. In the situation at that time his concern was that Confessing Church vicars and pastors remain true to the call that they had received to discipleship and the visible church in the form of the Confessing Church. Bonhoeffer for that reason discusses the burning topics of that historical moment, including love for one's enemy, the taking of loyalty oaths, or the right to resistance. The book, which was written in a radical, stern tone, views the Christians of that era at a fork in the road. Now it would be determined who would "walk with certainty the

---

16. DBWE 4:58–59.

narrow path of the church's decision," that is, whether to remain loyal to the decisions of the Barmen and Dahlem synods and, with that, to the one true visible church, and who would make the compromises that would lead to the abandonment of discipleship.[17]

Pressures on the Confessing Church

The Confessing Church's circumstances had become measurably more difficult during the first months of the preachers' seminary. After the beginning of 1935 the financial offices of the Old Prussian Union Church were under state control. Church disputes had to be dealt with by a division in the Interior Ministry. In addition, a Ministry for Church Affairs had been established with Hanns Kerrl as director, which immediately introduced church committees in which the different church factions were to work together. In this context Bonhoeffer signed a petition, "To Our Brothers in the Ministry,"[18] in which he made clear that these measures contradicted the decisions made in Barmen and Dahlem. Any opportunity to work in compromise with the state had to be rejected. Bonhoeffer viewed the readiness of many in the Confessing Church to work with bodies that had been created by the state as wrong. He wrote Martin Niemöller that "it is about time to create an Emergency League within the Emergency League."[19]

The preachers' seminary made numerous statements to Confessing Church leaders about church political issues, as on the occasion of the "Celebration of Resurrection" that the Nazi state scheduled on November 9, 1935, to commemorate the "martyrs" of the 1923 Beer Hall Putsch in Munich—for which the churches were to fly the state flags. The seminarians demanded that the Old Prussian Union Council of Brethren issue a "directive" that would make clear to Confessing Church pastors: "A clear confession on the occasion of this day would have to have consisted of a clear delimitation of the Christian hope in the resurrection from this ethnonationalistic [völkisch], idealistic idea of resurrection."[20]

The Fifth Implementation Decree of the Law to Restore Order in the German Evangelical Church had particularly far-reaching consequences for

---

17. DBWE 4:40.
18. DBWE 14:84–85.
19. DBWE 14:84.
20. DBWE 14:117.

the work of the Confessing Church. This decree, passed by the Ministry for Church Affairs on December 2, 1935, banned the Confessing Church from filling pastorates, announcing their activities, taking collections, and examining and ordaining pastors. After that, the preachers' seminaries were operating on the edges of illegality. Under these intensified circumstances the House of Brethren in Finkenwalde encouraged the former brothers: "Under no circumstances allow yourselves to be led astray by assertions that we are a "movement" rather than a church. Doing so abandons everything that was said in Barmen and Dahlem, and we end up alongside the faith *movement*, the German Christians. We are not a movement; we are the church of Jesus Christ."[21] While the Confessing synod that met February 17–22, 1936, in Bad Oeynhausen rejected any cooperation with the church committees that had been established by the Ministry for Church Affairs, it didn't completely forbid it. For within the Confessing Church the objection was raised that a ban on cooperation with state-related committees reflected Reformed "legalism" and that, from a Lutheran standpoint, such cooperation was legitimate within church regulations.[22] In contrast, Bonhoeffer argued that the regulations of the church existed for the sake of proclamation and had to be based purely on the church's confession. The church committees, he argued, were not legitimate because they had been established by an outside body and not by the church itself.

The Finkenwalde brotherhood and two other seminaries also protested in 1936 when more Confessing Church members (including some former Finkenwalde seminarians) opted to work with the committees:

It is horrifying to see how many of our colleagues who said yes to Barmen and Dahlem are now quietly refusing obedience to the Councils of Brethren and the Provisional Church Administration and are turning instead to the state committees. One cannot justify such a move on the basis of either Scripture or the confessions. Perhaps these people no longer even want to. This is nothing but undisciplined apostasy. . . . It was with faith and obedience alone that the church took up its prescribed battle. It took its guidance solely from the word. It was glad to give up all the worries, security, and friendship of the world for its Lord. . . . And today we want to deviate from it in exchange for the friendship of

21. DBWE 14:124.
22. DBWE 14:698.

the world? We want to sell our promise in exchange for the lentil stew of a secure future?! We are robbing our church's message of credibility through our own actions![23]

Bonhoeffer continued to be outspoken in his other church political positions. In the spring of 1936 he published an essay, "On the Question of Church Communion," in which he observed that the "Reich Church government has separated itself from the Christian church. The Confessing Church is the true church of Jesus Christ in Germany."[24] This meant that "[w]hoever knowingly separates himself from the Confessing Church in Germany separates himself from salvation."[25] This sentence provoked a bitter debate. Bonhoeffer noted that if the Confessing Church were not the only true church,

> . . . it is difficult to understand why young theologians should risk their very existence in order to be examined, ordained, and appointed by the Confessing Church. The suffering of imprisoned and expelled brothers for the sake of this cause is then no longer suffering for the sake of Christ and Christ's cause. . . . Either the Barmen Declaration is a true confession to the Lord Jesus effected by the Holy Spirit, in which case its character can be constructive or schismatic for the church; or it is a nonbinding expression of the opinion of several different theologians, and the Confessing Church itself has since then been traveling down a fateful, false path.[26]

Bonhoeffer's starkly critical statement was not intended to exclude people from salvation, however, but to shame the German Christian church leadership. The congregation was affected "only to the extent it adheres *knowingly* to false teachers. As long as the legitimate possibility remains that they might be convinced otherwise, we count them as members of the legitimate church and address them as those who still belong to us."[27] In March 1936 Bonhoeffer traveled with the Finkenwalde seminarians to Denmark and Sweden, invited by the Swedish ecumenical council. The journey drew quite a bit of attention

---

23. DBWE 14:190–91.
24. DBWE 14:668.
25. DBWE 14:675.
26. DBWE 14:691, 694.
27. DBWE 14:211.

ecumenically, and Foreign Office bishop Theodor Heckel wrote a warning to the state church committee in Pomerania: "Because one could charge him with being both a pacifist and an enemy of the state, the Regional Church Committee might be well advised to dissociate itself from him and to take measures to ensure that he will no longer train German theologians."[28] For some time the state had been aware that Bonhoeffer should not be permitted to direct a virtually illegal preachers' seminary and at the same time have an adjunct position at the University in Berlin. On August 5, 1936, his right to teach at the University was revoked by the Reich and Prussian Ministry for Science, Training, and Public Education, which stated this reason (and also mentioned the trip to Sweden).[29]

Throughout his work at Finkenwalde, Bonhoeffer informed ecumenical representatives overseas about the German situation and tried to build a regular ecumenical conversation between Confessing Church candidates and foreign churches, for the purpose also of gaining outside support. He insisted

that in every dialogue with it (the Confessing Church), the element of church solidarity comes to expression insofar as its dialogue partner not enter into simultaneous dialogue with the Confessing Church and with the churches of false doctrine rejected by the Confessing Church; indeed, insofar as its ecumenical dialogue partners definitively break off discussion, the Confessing Church itself, in its own responsibility as a church, declares such discussions to be broken off.[30]

For the most part, this demand met with little support abroad. People suspected that behind Bonhoeffer's demands was "a theology that declares itself to be absolute."[31] Bonhoeffer and the other Confessing Church representatives remained firm, declining to attend the meetings of the World Alliance and ecumenical council in August 1935 in Chamby, because representatives of the Reich church had been invited.

One year later, however, Bonhoeffer did attend an ecumenical council in Chamby. There were renewed debates about the procedures for German

---

28. DBWE 14:148.
29. DBWE 14:231.
30. DBWE 14:388–89.
31. In the words of Hans Schönfeld, the director of the Research Department for the Ecumenical Office for Life and Work; DBWE 14:68.

attendance. Finally, three German delegations took part: one from the Confessing Church, one from the Lutheran Council that had been founded in 1934, and one from the Reich church. Resigned in light of the lack of ecumenical clarity, Bonhoeffer said nothing at the conference.

On August 29, 1937, Heinrich Himmler, head of the SS, banned the preachers' seminaries. Finkenwalde was closed by the Gestapo on September 28, 1937.

CHAPTER EIGHT

THE PATH INTO ILLEGALITY, 1937–1940

The New Form of Seminary

The fifth session in Finkenwalde ended on September 11, 1937—two weeks after Himmler's ban on the training of vicars by the Confessing Church.

Bonhoeffer continued to train vicars, however. The ever-more frequent arrests of Protestant and Catholic pastors made him well aware of the growing risks of this activity. On July 1, 1937, even Martin Niemöller, one of the most prominent leaders of the Confessing Church, had been arrested. Bonhoeffer wrote his brother Karl-Friedrich in November 1937 about his mother's growing worries about his work:

> I'm always sorry when Mother gets so worried and then also draws others into her worries. But there really is no reason for it. Really, we can't *allow* ourselves to worry about whether as a result of Himmler's edict I may meet the same fate hundreds of others already have. We will not be able to persevere on behalf of the church without making sacrifices. After all, you yourselves risked significantly more during the war. Why should we not do the same for the church? And why would anyone want to dissuade

us from doing so? Certainly none of us is particularly keen on going to prison, but if it does happen, then—at least I would hope—we will do so with joy precisely because the cause is worthwhile. At the beginning of next week we will be starting again.[1]

At the beginning of December 1937 the training of vicars continued in two Pomeranian parsonages, one in Köslin and the other in Groß-Schlönwitz. The second group was moved in April 1939 to nearby Sigurdshof, since the parsonage in Groß-Schlönwitz was needed by the new pastor. These were "collective pastorates" in which the candidates were officially registered as "apprentice vicars," serving pastors who still had official pastorates but were members of the Confessing Church. The candidates assisted in the congregations, but for the most part lived together in the two parsonages so that they could participate in a community similar to that in Finkenwalde—which, of course, had to remain secret. In each of the parsonages six to nine candidates lived together for a half year; there were a total of five such groups. The collective pastorate in Köslin for the winter of 1939–40 was cancelled due to the beginning of the war and the military conscription of most of the candidates.

Eberhard Bethge became inspector of studies in Groß-Schlönwitz, Fritz Onnasch in Köslin. The collective pastorates were supported by the two church superintendents who oversaw these districts. Fritz Onnasch's father, Friedrich, was superintendent in Köslin; in Schlawe (the district where Groß-Schlönwitz was located) Eduard Block was superintendent. Both superintendents assumed the responsibility for the vicars toward both state and church offices. Block formally assigned Bonhoeffer to be assistant pastor.

Bonhoeffer repeated the lectures he had offered in Finkenwalde. The candidates found this period deeply moving. As one of them later wrote Bonhoeffer:

I did not come to Schlönwitz gladly and full of hope. . . . I looked toward this period of physical and spiritual confinement with a shudder. To me it was a necessary evil, into which one had to enter with good grace and for the sake of self-discipline had to get through with good grace. . . . all turned out quite differently than I had feared. Instead of coming into the stuffy air of theological bigotry, I entered a world that united many things that I love and need: accurate theological work on the common ground of fellowship, in which one's own inabilities were never noticed

---

1. DBWE 14:320–21.

in a hurtful fashion, but rather which turned work into pleasure; true fellowship under the Word that united all "without respect to person"— and nonetheless with open-mindedness and love for everything that makes even this fallen creation still worthy of love: music, literature, sports, and the beauty of the earth. . . .[2]

After the educational work had been officially forbidden, Bonhoeffer wrote every "circular letter" himself, addressed to each as a "personal letter."

Bonhoeffer's own situation was becoming increasingly difficult. On January 11, 1938, after he participated in a Confessing Church gathering in Berlin that the Gestapo incorrectly believed was a theological lecture (these had been banned), he and the other attendees from outside the city were prohibited from traveling to Berlin. After his father appealed the ruling, he was permitted an exemption for family visits.

Life Together

After the closing of Finkenwalde, Bonhoeffer wrote a book on his concept of collective spiritual life and published it in 1939 under the title *Gemeinsames Leben* [ET: *Life Together*]. His Finkenwalde experiment had not been "a concern of some private circles but . . . a mission entrusted to the church."[3] Like *Discipleship*, *Life Together* was to find a wide audience in numerous languages.

One of the very first sentences in the book expresses the pressures of the Church Struggle: "the Christian cannot simply take for granted the privilege of living among other Christians. . . . Christians belong not in the seclusion of a cloistered life but in the midst of enemies. There they find their mission, their work."[4] To be able to live together with other Christians—as was the case in Finkenwalde—is grace. It was important to Bonhoeffer that the fellowship with other Christians was not sought for the sake of human company but for the sake of Jesus Christ: "Christians need other Christians who speak God's Word to them. They need them again and again when they become uncertain and disheartened because, living by their own resources, they cannot help themselves without cheating themselves out of the truth. . . . The Christ in one's own heart is uncertain; the Christ in the word of another Christian is

---

2. DBWE 15:127–28.
3. DBWE 5:25.
4. DBWE 5:27.

certain."[5] Christian fellowship was neither an ideal that needed to be brought to reality nor a psychological community driven by emotional affection. It already exists when each individual member of the Christian community believes in Jesus Christ. Thus it is ultimately constituted through Christ, and this should be the basis for its form.

For Bonhoeffer, the daily routine in the Christian community had to include both communal and individual elements. The day began together with worship in the early morning: "A community living together gathers for praise and thanks, Scripture reading, and prayer. The profound silence of morning is first broken by the prayer and song of the community of faith. . . . For Christians the beginning of the day should not be burdened and haunted by the various kinds of concerns they face during the working day."[6] Bonhoeffer made specific suggestions for structuring such a morning worship: first the praying of a psalm, then a hymn, followed by a scriptural reading using a longer excerpt from both the Old and New Testaments. This should be followed by singing, and the service should conclude with free prayer. Evenings ended with another communal devotion.

Individual confession of sin, in which one brother confessed his sins to another, had special significance for the community:

> In confession there takes place a *breakthrough to community*. Sin wants to be alone with people. It takes them away from the community. The more lonely people become, the more destructive the power of sin over them. The more deeply they become entangled in it, the more unholy is their loneliness. Sin wants to remain unknown. It shuns the light. In the darkness of what is left unsaid sin poisons the whole being of a person.[7]

Yet when sin is confessed before another it loses its power. Instead of easily forgiving ourselves, in confessing to another we take the first step toward ending our sin.

At the same time, Bonhoeffer stressed, "*Whoever cannot be alone should beware of community*,"[8] but the reverse was also true: "Each taken by itself has profound pitfalls and perils. Those who want community without solitude

---

5. DBWE 5:32; trans. altered.
6. DBWE 5:51.
7. DBWE 5:110.
8. DBWE 5:82.

plunge into the void of words and feelings, and those who seek solitude without community perish in the bottomless pit of vanity, self-infatuation, and despair."[9] Correct solitude is indicated by silence, above all before and after listening to the biblical word. In the daily meditation period we should open ourselves to the biblical text, waiting and listening for what it says to us. This is explicitly not to be a period of self-observation or self-reflection: "there is no more time to observe ourselves in meditation than there is in the Christian life as a whole."[10] Intercessory prayer is particularly important in the meditation period:

> A Christian community either lives by the intercessory prayers of its members for one another, or the community will be destroyed. I can no longer condemn or hate other Christians for whom I pray, no matter how much trouble they cause me. In intercessory prayer the face that may have been strange and intolerable to me is transformed into the face of one for whom Christ died, the face of a pardoned sinner.[11]

The person can tell whether the experience of community and solitude was good if she or he emerges from it with courage, free and strengthened for the day's work.

The Crisis of the Confessing Church

The Confessing Church entered a difficult crisis after all the pastors in the Old Prussian Union church were told to swear a loyalty oath to Adolf Hitler on the occasion of his birthday on April 20, 1938. According to the director of the Church Chancellery in Berlin, pastors who held office could continue to do so only if they stood "in steadfast loyalty to Führer, Volk and Reich." The wording of the oath was: "I swear that I will be faithful and obedient to Adolf Hitler, the Führer of the German Reich and people, that I will conscientiously observe the laws and carry out the duties of my office, so help me God."[12] Whoever declined to take the oath was to be dismissed.

---

9. DBWE 5:83.
10. DBWE 5:88.
11. DBWE 5:90.
12. Cited in Eberhard Bethge, *Dietrich Bonhoeffer: A Biography*, trans. Eric Mosbacher, et al., rev. and ed. Victoria J. Barnett (Minneapolis: Fortress Press, 2000), 600.

There was no unanimity in the Confessing Church about what to do. Was this a state requirement that one simply had to follow, or a church demand from the illegitimate church leadership that one had to refuse? At its second meeting in Berlin-Steglitz, the sixth Confessing synod of the Old Prussian Union decided that the oath had to be taken because it was a state order. Later, when most pastors had already taken the oath, it became clear that the National Socialist leadership viewed it as a purely internal church matter; this infuriated many, including Bonhoeffer.

Bonhoeffer, who was not a pastor appointed to a congregation, was not affected by the order. But he took a clear position: when the synod had directed pastors to take the oath, it had infringed both on their individual freedom of conscience and on brotherly love for the weak:

> The rift thereby brought about in the Confessing Church is—in human terms—irreparable. . . . I can only regard the guilt that the Confessing Church has taken upon itself, through the "*directive*" to take the oath, as the outcome of a path where a lack of authority, gladness in confession, courage of faith, and readiness to suffer has been evident for some time.[13]

Because of this and other critiques, Bonhoeffer's position in the Confessing Church was becoming more and more an isolated one. He dismissed another compromise—the attempt immediately after this crisis to improve relations between the Confessing Church, the "intact" Lutheran churches in Württemberg and Bavaria, and the so-called neutral church leaders through a "Proposal for Regulation for the Appointment of a Church Administration"—because, among other reasons, it made no reference to Barmen and Dahlem. They were negotiating in opposition to "God's clear directive."[14] After the loyalty oath crisis "we had indeed expected a different, more spiritual statement from our church authorities. What has now been advised to us is the self-surrender of the Confessing Church. Here we will no longer follow."[15]

On November 9, 1938, the pogrom during which Jewish synagogues, homes, and businesses were destroyed, Bonhoeffer underlined the words of Psalm 74:8b in his Bible: "They burned all the meeting places of God in the land" and noted the date, "9.11.38," in the margins. He also put a line and an

---

13. DBWE 15:57.
14. DBWE 15:67.
15. DBWE 15:67.

explanation mark in the margins next to it: "We do not see our signs; there is no longer any prophet, and there is none among us who knows how long"—a clear expression that in this dramatic situation he no longer expected much of his church. While Bonhoeffer said nothing publicly, there were a few individuals in the Confessing Church, such as Elisabeth Schmitz and Julius von Jan, who took public stands and suffered the consequences.

The Confessing Church's position had become less and less clear, and Bonhoeffer felt besieged by the questions from his former seminarians as to what they should now do. Bonhoeffer urged them to continue consequently on the path they had chosen. In a "personal letter" to them in November 1938 he wrote:

> We think that we are acting particularly responsibly when every few weeks we reconsider the question of whether the path on which we've started was the right one. Here it's especially striking that such "responsible examination" always commences just when serious difficulties become evident. We then convince ourselves that we no longer have "the right gladness and certainty for this path" or, even worse, that God is no longer with us with his word in the old clarity, and with all this we essentially are only trying to circumvent that which the New Testament calls "patient endurance" and "probation." In any case, Paul did not begin to reflect about whether his path was right when obstacles and suffering threatened, nor did Luther; instead, in the very midst of this they may have become completely certain and joyful, standing in discipleship and communion with their lord. Dear brothers, our real crisis is not at all the doubt about the path we have begun but rather our failure of patience, of remaining below.[16]

Bonhoeffer was all the more upset whenever he learned that one of his former Finkenwalde seminarians had chosen legalization, that is, the return to official status under the Consistory of the German Protestant Church. One seminarian explained his decision to Bonhoeffer as follows:

> Certainly the altered circumstances had their say as well, namely, the fact that many one-time GC [German Christians] today are fine preachers, that the church government, the consistory, today is less heretical

---

16. DBWE 15:82.

than tyrannical. . . . What finally gave me pause was the insight that on this path I would have to give up the established church, because my work would remain possible only within the circles of CC [Confessing Church] congregations. I believed, however, that the abandonment of the established church was not yet commanded, but rather that today the waiting of which Luke 13:6-9 speaks must still hold true. For I know that I am called to serve in these congregations, for their admonition and edification, not only to serve CC circles. . . . Finally I had to see that the "path to the consistory" would not necessarily have to be a repudiation and an acting without faith. My personal negotiations in these weeks, which are not yet completely finished, have confirmed this. Certainly the men there are "tied down" and theologically poorly qualified for church leadership. But they require nothing for legalization that I would have to reject as "against the faith" or "against the truth." If this is true, then the protest against the consistory at this point loses for me that necessity that it ought to have, if I were to renounce for its sake the ministry, the established church, the fellowship with many brothers who share my faith, etc., and to bear all the suffering. . . . Thus I see—assuming that my negotiations with the consistory proceed unhindered—no more possibility of remaining on the previous path of the CC. Whether I remain *in* the CC is for the CC to decide; whether I remain in the Finkenwalde brotherhood, that is my request and question to you.[17]

The answer for Bonhoeffer was clear. In his next circular letter to the brothers he spoke of the "pain that several brothers have abandoned our cause," emphasizing that the brothers should stand "in clear and firm community with those who are committed to the same cause."[18]

He felt that the situation of the Confessing Church improved somewhat with the seventh Old Prussian Union Confessing synod in Berlin-Nikolassee in January 1939, which finally made a clear statement against cooperation with state-appointed church officials. Bonhoeffer reacted with relief: "The new beginning that has recently been given to us through God's goodness against all expectations has liberated us from a dull pressure."[19]

---

17. DBWE 15:150–51.
18. DBWE 15:166.
19. DBWE 15:144.

A Way Out in the United States?

At the beginning of September 1938 Bonhoeffer's twin sister Sabine emigrated with her husband, Gerhard Leibholz, first to Switzerland and then to London; he, like all other "non-Aryans" was the object of increasing repressive measures. Bonhoeffer visited the family in London in March 1939, and for the first time met Willem Visser 't Hooft, general secretary of the World Council of Churches, which was in the process of formation. A friendship marked by trust quickly developed between the two men, which would have special significance for Bonhoeffer in the political conspiracy of the years that followed. During his five-week stay in England Bonhoeffer also met again with Bishop George Bell, telling him of the latest developments in the church but also asking his personal advice. As he wrote Bell shortly before they met:

> I am thinking of leaving Germany sometime. The main reason is the compulsory military service to which the men of my age (1906) will be called up this year. It seems to me conscientiously impossible to join in a war under the present circumstances. On the other hand, the Confessional Church as such has not taken any definite attitude in this respect and probably cannot take it as things are. So I should cause a tremendous damage to my brethren if I would make a stand on this point which would be regarded by the regime as typical of the hostility of our church towards the state. Perhaps the worst thing of all is the military oath which I should have to swear . . . as things are I should have to do violence to my Christian conviction, if I would take up arms "now and here."[20]

After speaking with Bell, Bonhoeffer met with Reinhold Niebuhr, his former professor from the New York period. Niebuhr immediately got in touch with Paul Lehmann and Henry Smith Leiper, the ecumenical general secretary of the Federal Council of Churches in New York, asking them to invite Bonhoeffer to the United States. The idea was for him to work for a time in the church and academic spheres, also for the sake of maintaining ecumenical ties to the Confessing Church. On May 28, 1939, Bonhoeffer was given a leave of absence at his own request from his work in the illegal collective pastorates. The work was to continue, but at that point a successor had not yet been named.

---

20. DBWE 15:156–57; the prose reflects Bonhoeffer's English.

On June 2 Bonhoeffer left for New York with his brother Karl-Friedrich via London. It was not easy for him to leave Germany. In a note he sent to Bethge during the flight over the English Channel, "My thoughts are between you all and the future. Take care of yourself. Greet all the brothers. They are now holding the evening service! God with you all!"[21]

Bonhoeffer was already having doubts about whether he had made the right decision on the boat to the United States. He continually thought about the situation in Germany and the situation of the Finkenwalde brothers. In his travel diary, Bonhoeffer wrote (in the second person plural, thinking of the entire community he had left behind in Pomerania):

> Today is Sunday. No worship service. Moreover, the hours have already shifted so that I cannot take part in your worship as it is happening. But I am fully with you, today more than ever. If only the doubts about my own path were overcome. The own search for the secrets of the heart, which are unfathomable—"for God knows the secrets of our heart." When the confusion of reproaches and excuses, of wishes and fears makes everything in us opaque, God sees in all clarity right through to the bottom. There, however, God finds the very name that he himself has inscribed: Jesus Christ.[22]

Once he had arrived in the United States, Bonhoeffer had a series of conversations about meaningful work there. It would be possible to give summer classes and lectures. Leiper offered him a position overseeing German refugees, which would have made an early return to Germany impossible for Bonhoeffer. He was internally torn by the signs of war and concerns about Germany: "Disturbing political news from Japan. If turmoil now breaks out, I will definitely travel to Germany. I cannot be alone abroad. That is utterly clear to me. I do live over there, after all."[23] Bonhoeffer reached his conclusion in a conversation with Leiper on June 20: "Visit with Leiper. With that the decision has been made. I turned it down. He was visibly disappointed and indeed somewhat put out. For me it may mean something more than I

---

21. DBWE 15:175; trans. altered.
22. DBWE 15:219.
23. DBWE 15:223.

Dietrich Bonhoeffer with his twin sister Sabine Leibholz in 1939 in London, after his return from the United States

am able to foresee at the moment. God alone knows."[24] Bonhoeffer wrote to Niebuhr apologetically:

> I have come to the conclusion that I have made a mistake in coming to America. I must live through this difficult period of our national history with the Christian people of Germany. I will have no right to participate in the reconstruction of Christian life in Germany after the war if I do not share the trials of this time with my people. My brothers in the Confessional Synod wanted me to go. They may have been right in urging me to do so; but I was wrong in going. Such a decision each man must make for himself. Christians in Germany will face the terrible alternative of either willing the defeat of their nation in order that Christian civilization may survive, or willing the victory of their nation and thereby

---

24. DBWE 15:227.

destroying our civilization. I know which of these alternatives I must choose; but I cannot make that choice in security . . .[25]

On July 7 Bonhoeffer and his brother boarded the ship back to Germany, via London. Upon arrival he immediately returned to Pomerania to resume work with the collective pastorates. Bonhoeffer led a session in Sigurdshof for the last time, until the Gestapo closed it on March 18, 1940. Six months earlier, only a few weeks after Bonhoeffer had returned to Germany, Hitler's army marched into Poland, starting the Second World War on September 1, 1939.

---

25. DBWE 15:210; Niebuhr's wording.

CHAPTER NINE

The Conspiracy Period, 1940–1943

Preparations for a Coup

Even before his trip to the United States, Bonhoeffer's brother-in-law Hans von Dohnanyi had informed Bonhoeffer of the coup being planned in the Office of Military Intelligence in the Army High Command, involving Admiral Wilhelm Canaris and General Hans Oster. Dohnanyi had been working in the political division of Military Intelligence since August 25, 1939, and was able to help Bonhoeffer avoid military service by getting him an assignment to the overseas desk of Military Intelligence in Munich. Bonhoeffer received a "UK" military classification, which exempted him from active military duty by declaring him indispensable as a civilian for the war effort. The official reason given was that Bonhoeffer's ecumenical contacts might be useful in helping the Military Intelligence office obtain information from abroad. Bonhoeffer's role, in fact, went in the opposite direction: he was able to convey information to his contacts abroad, specifically to tell his trusted ecumenical allies of the coup plans. Josef Müller, a legal counselor in the Military Intelligence office, had the same assignment with respect to the Vatican. The conspirators hoped the knowledge that there was a serious resistance group in Germany that was also planning for a postwar German government would prevent the Allied nations, in the event of a successful overthrow of Hitler, from destroying Germany.

In the following years Bonhoeffer traveled three times to Switzerland as well as to Norway with Helmuth James Graf von Moltke (who worked for Military Intelligence as well), and to Sweden and Italy. Bonhoeffer discussed the political situation and the coup plans with different church leaders, also speaking with them about the church's task during the war and the eventual postwar reconstruction. Bonhoeffer met with various contacts, including Karl Barth in Zurich, Willem Visser 't Hooft in Geneva, George Bell in Sigtuna, Sweden, and with representatives of the church resistance in Norway. Acting on behalf of General Ludwig Beck, Bonhoeffer shared with Bell the names of the most important conspirators. The Canaris-Oster resistance circles were hoping for a signal from the Allies that in the event of a coup the Allies would not militarily take over Germany—a signal that could move reluctant German military leaders to join in the coup. Bell's efforts to convince British leaders of the hoped-for solidarity failed; Allied leaders were waiting for more reliable proof of German opposition.

Bonhoeffer's sudden appearance as a staff member in the Military Intelligence and his travel abroad with the permission of the National Socialist regime sparked unavoidable distrust and irritation among his foreign conversation partners. How could this be a man of the Confessing Church? In May 1942 Bonhoeffer heard the rumor that Karl Barth was upset about it; Bonhoeffer for his part was deeply troubled by this news and wrote Barth: "In a time in which so much simply has to rest on personal trust, *everything* is lost if mistrust arises. I can, of course, understand that this curse of suspicion gradually afflicts us all, but it is difficult to bear when for the first time it affects oneself personally."[1] Barth's theological assistant, Charlotte von Kirschbaum, assured Bonhoeffer immediately on Barth's behalf: "Karl Barth has never mistrusted you for a second."[2] The story shows that even long friendships suffered under the difficult political situation.

After the deportations of Jews from Berlin began in October 1941, the Office of Military Intelligence attempted to help a small group of people who faced deportation to concentration camps[3]. The so-called "Operation Seven" brought them to safety in Switzerland, under the guise of being

---

1. DBWE 16:278.
2. DBWE 16:279.
3. Eleven were "non-Aryan Christians"; three were secular Jews.

counterintelligence informants. While Bonhoeffer did not play a role person-ally, he saw to it that Charlotte Friedenthal, an important Confessing Church staff member, was one of those rescued, and this act would come up during his later interrogations in prison. In addition, Bonhoeffer and lawyer Friedrich Perels, who was also involved in the resistance, compiled extensive documen-tation about the deportations and sent it to Dohnanyi to pass on to German military leaders.[4]

Bonhoeffer also wrestled personally with the question of German recon-struction after the war ended, particularly with respect to what the church's role might be. Like many of those in the political resistance he set his hopes not on a democracy, given the experience of the Weimar Republic, but on a strong government that would reflect the God-given duties of the state: "No form of the state is as such an absolute guarantee of a proper performance of the office of government. Only concrete obedience to the divine task justifies a form of the state. . . . The relatively best form of the state will be that in which it is most clear that government is from above, from God, and in which its divine origin shines through most brightly."[5] Bonhoeffer drafted a church announcement to be read after the successful coup; it spoke of guilt, repen-tance, and personal confession, of forgiveness and renewal.[6]

In 1942 Bonhoeffer became involved with the Freiburg circle, a group of experts from various fields who were drafting suggestions for the restructuring of different German institutions and organizations after the war; this became known as the Freiburg memorandum. He made various suggestions but was not involved in actually drafting it. On September 8, 1944, Constantin von Dietze, one of the leaders of the circle, was arrested and charged with pre-paring for the coup through his plans for the reorganization of Germany; Bonhoeffer was cited in the indictment of von Dietze as having initiated the memorandum.[7]

Ethics

Bonhoeffer's short book, *Das Gebetbuch der Bibel. Eine Einführung in die Psalmen* [ET: *The Prayerbook of the Bible: An Introduction to the Psalms*],

---

4. DBWE 16:225–29.
5. DBWE 16:527.
6. DBWE 16:572–74.
7. DBWE 16:467.

appeared in 1940; it was Bonhoeffer's reading of the Psalms from the perspective of Jesus Christ. Bonhoeffer wrote that these were ultimately the prayers of Jesus Christ and are therefore Christian prayers: "Who prays the Psalter? David . . . prays. Christ prays. We pray. . . . David, Christ, the congregation, I myself—wherever we consider all these things with one another, we become aware of the wonderful path that God follows in order to teach us to pray . . ."[8] For Bonhoeffer, this deeply Jewish text was "the prayer book of Jesus Christ in the truest sense of the word."[9] With this, Bonhoeffer was explicitly opposing the exclusion of the Old Testament and Judaism.

On March 19, 1941, he was "forbidden every activity as a writer."[10] He had already been banned from public speaking due to "activity subverting the people";[11] in addition, Bonhoeffer was required to appear regularly at the police office in Schlawe, Pomerania. All these restricted his movements.

Despite the ban on writing Bonhoeffer continued his theological work, primarily on his *Ethics* (Ger.: *Ethik*). He returned constantly to this manuscript in which he wanted to draft an ethic for the period following the war. From November 1940 to February 1941 he retreated to concentrate on it in the Benedictine monastery in Ettal, Bavaria. Because of his arrest on April 4, 1943, he was unable to complete the manuscript.

The draft of a new ethic was extraordinarily important for Bonhoeffer. As he wrote Bethge from prison: "I . . . sometimes think my life is more or less behind me and all I have left to do is to complete my *Ethics*."[12] Bethge hid the manuscript that lay on Bonhoeffer's desk after the latter's arrest. After Bonhoeffer's death he put the various manuscripts in order and published them in 1949.[13] The book only drew attention after the publication of Bonhoeffer's prison letters, however.

In the fragmentary text Bonhoeffer left behind it is clear he wanted to give a new foundation for Christian ethics. For Bonhoeffer, the starting point for Christian ethics is the reconciliation between God and humanity, which has already taken place in Jesus Christ. This starting point gives the work its

---

8. DBWE 5:160.
9. DBWE 5:54–55.
10. DBWE 16:182.
11. DBWE 16:71.
12. DBWE 8:222.
13. Bonhoeffer scholars have proven Bethge's original ordering of the manuscripts to be unlikely and they have been published in the Bonhoeffer Works series in a different order that reflects the true chronology of the texts.

understanding of God and the world. God and the world are not two separate realities; rather,

> *In Jesus Christ the reality of God has entered into the reality of this world. . . .* In Christ we are invited to participate in the reality of God and the reality of the world at the same time, the one not without the other. The reality of God is disclosed only as it places me completely into the reality of the world. But I find the reality of the world always already borne, accepted, and reconciled in the reality of God.[14]

Christian ethics must start with this unity of God and the world in Jesus Christ. In the first instance, this unity means that the Christian "is no longer the person of eternal conflict. . . . Worldliness does not separate one from Christ, and being Christian does not separate one from the world. Belonging completely to Christ, one stands at the same time completely in the world."[15] Furthermore, it means that ethics asks, "how the reality in Christ—which has long embraced us and our world within itself—works here and now or, in other words, how life is to be lived in it."[16] Bonhoeffer did not find the concentration on Jesus Christ as too narrow; rather, "The more exclusively we recognize and confess Christ as our Lord, the more will be disclosed to us the breadth of Christ's lordship."[17]

The category of responsibility has particular significance for Bonhoeffer in *Ethics*. It picks up on his previously expressed conviction that human action should not derive from general principles, but had to be directed each time at the concrete situation. Particularly in the face of the "masks in which evil approaches"[18]—in which evil poses as the good, helpful, necessary, and just, Bonhoeffer believed that the traditional ethical concepts of reason, conscience, duty, or virtue were no longer helpful. The person who is grounded in reason might not grasp the abyss of evil. The one for whom conscience is the decisive motive would be overwhelmed by the complexity of decisions he or she faced, none of which would give him or her a good conscience. To take duty as the primary motive is only dangerous: "People of duty must finally

---

14. DBWE 6:54–55.
15. DBWE 6:62.
16. DBWE 6:55.
17. DBWE 6:344.
18. DBWE 6:79.

fulfill their duty even to the devil."[19] And the person for whom personal virtue is the highest value will find that in a situation of widespread injustice, in which action on behalf of one virtue conflicts with another, she or he can only retreat into the private sphere.

In a text written for his co-conspirators at the end of 1942 Bonhoeffer takes up these thoughts again, and concludes with the question of whether anyone is in the situation to withstand the "masquerade of evil":[20]

> Who stands firm? Only the one whose ultimate standard is not his reason, his principles, conscience . . . or virtue; only the one who is prepared to sacrifice all of these when, in faith and in relationship to God alone, he is called to obedient and responsible action. Such a person is the responsible one, whose life is to be nothing but a response to God's question and call. Where are these responsible ones?[21]

It is striking that in the *Ethics*, in which the immediate political situation and his involvement in the violent resistance movement stand unspoken in the background, Bonhoeffer does not reach the conclusion that there are situations in which it is permissible to kill, that is, act in disobedience to the Fifth Commandment. This would have categorized the murder of Hitler as ethically unproblematic. Instead, Bonhoeffer's reply to the most pressing conflict facing the conspirators is this: there could be an "extraordinary situation"[22] that appeals to "the freedom of those who act responsibly," which means that one's own action infringes on God's law and with that one deliberately becomes guilty. Such action is only possible in the context of faith in God's forgiveness:

> Extraordinary necessity appeals to the freedom of those who act responsibly. In this case there is no law behind which they could take cover. Therefore there is also no law that, in the face of such necessity, could force them to make this rather than that particular decision. Instead, in such a situation, one must completely let go of any law, knowing that here one must decide as a free venture. This must also include the open

---

19. DBWE 6:79.
20. DBWE 8:38.
21. DBWE 8:40.
22. DBWE 6:273.

acknowledgment that here the law is being broken, violated . . . thereby affirming the legitimacy of the law in the very act of violating it . . .[23]

When the person decides whether to obey the law (that is, the divine law not to kill) or not to obey it, "in either case one becomes guilty, and is able to live only by divine grace and forgiveness."[24] Two further considerations are important for Bonhoeffer's *Ethics*: the distinction between ultimate and penultimate things, and the affirmation of the four mandates.

Following an idea of Martin Luther, Bonhoeffer names four mandates that God has established in the world. He is referring to four distinct divinely given duties that give structure to the reality of the world and are intended to preserve it for Christ: work (or culture); marriage and family; government; and church. According to Bonhoeffer, human beings are to live under these mandates; the quality of their content is given through their directedness toward Christ. His explication of the duties of government is interesting; for Bonhoeffer, government exists for the protection of marriage and work, but not (here the historical context is clear) in order to shape them on behalf of its own interests. None of the mandates may be set as absolutes. They fulfill their functions "only in their being with-one-another, for-one-another, and over-against-one-another."[25]

Bonhoeffer's distinction between ultimate and penultimate introduces an important differentiation about free human action: the ultimate is God's mercy on the sinner, which human beings cannot bring about through good deeds; it remains a gift after the human has acted. People can hope for it but not count on it. The significance of the penultimate is for the sake of the ultimate; it is that which needs God's mercy. Ethical action occurs in the realm of the penultimate, but with a view to the ultimate, for the penultimate must be preserved and formed for the sake of the ultimate. Ethical action in the penultimate is never done in order to constitute ultimate reality, but it may also not neglect the penultimate for the sake of the ultimate:

The hungry person needs bread, the homeless person needs shelter, the one deprived of rights needs justice, the lonely person needs community, the undisciplined one needs order, and the slave needs freedom. It would

---

23. DBWE 6:274.
24. DBWE 6:274.
25. DBWE 6:393.

be blasphemy against God and our neighbor to leave the hungry unfed while saying that God is closest to those in deepest need. We break bread with the hungry and share our home with them for the sake of Christ's love, which belongs to the hungry as much as it does to us. . . . What happens here is something penultimate. To give the hungry bread is not yet to proclaim to them the grace of God and justification, and to have received bread does not yet mean to stand in faith. But for the one who does something penultimate for the sake of the ultimate, this penultimate thing is related to the ultimate. It is a *pen*-ultimate, before the last. The entry of grace is the ultimate.[26]

"Dear Miss von Wedemeyer"

Bonhoeffer had been in a close friendship since 1925 with Elisabeth Zinn, a distant relative in Berlin. From the time of his break with her in 1933 to the closing of the House of Brethren in 1937, Bonhoeffer wasn't in a close relationship with a woman. Under the circumstances of the Church Struggle this was undoubtedly a relief, since he was freed from family ties and could devote himself completely to his duties, without fear of doing harm to a wife or children through his acts. This was also the way of life he recommended to the other men in the House of Brethren.

The year 1942 brought about a decisive personal turning point, and he began to see Maria von Wedemeyer, the granddaughter of Ruth von Kleist-Retzow, in a new light. Maria von Wedemeyer was the daughter of the attorney and officer Hans von Wedemeyer and Ruth von Kleist-Retzow's daughter Ruth; she had grown up on the family estate in Pätzig (in the Neumark region of Mark Brandenburg) with her six siblings before attending boarding schools in Thuringia and Baden. She and Bonhoeffer had met earlier through her grandmother, and in 1938 Bonhoeffer confirmed her brother Max. They met again in Klein-Krössin in June 1942 after Bonhoeffer's return from Sweden. Maria von Wedemeyer later described the encounter:

> I had just graduated from high school and was paying some family visits before embarking on my national service year at the boarding school in Altenburg. Foremost among these visits was one to my grandmother, to whom I had always been especially close. The feeling was mutual,

---

26. DBWE 6:163.

because she thought I resembled her as a young girl. I had been there a week when the celebrated Pastor Bonhoeffer came to stay. I was a bit put out at first, to be honest, but it very soon emerged that the three of us got on extremely well together. The other two conversed in such a way that I not only felt I understood what they were talking about but was cordially encouraged to join in. Which I did. I'm afraid I used to take a cocky tone with my grandmother, which amused her, and which I maintained even when Dietrich turned up. We talked about future plans. Grandmother pronounced my plan to study mathematics a silly whim, but Dietrich, perhaps for that very reason, took it seriously. We went for a stroll in the garden. He said he'd been to America, and we noted with surprise that I'd never before met anyone who had been there.[27]

Despite the significant difference in their ages—he was 36, she was 18—Bonhoeffer fell in love with her. In the months that followed they saw each other on different occasions. In August 1942 Maria von Wedemeyer's father,

Maria von Wedemeyer in 1942

27. Ruth-Alice von Bismarck and Ulrich Kabitz, eds., *Love Letters from Cell 92: The Correspondence between Dietrich Bonhoeffer and Maria von Wedemeyer*, trans. John Brownjohn (Nashville: Abingdon, 1995), 329–30.

Hans, was killed in Russia; the death of her brother Max on the eastern front followed in October. Bonhoeffer wrote her after her brother's death:

> Dear Miss von Wedemeyer, If I might be allowed to say only this to you, I believe I have an inkling of what Max's death means for you. It can scarcely help to tell you I too share in this pain. At such times it can only help us to cast ourselves upon the heart of God, not with words but truly and entirely. This requires many difficult hours, day and night, but when we have let go entirely into God—or better, when God has received us— then we are helped.[28]

It was difficult for the two to get to know one another better. Bonhoeffer had told Wedemeyer very quickly of his feelings for her. While her grand-mother supported the growing relationship, her mother was concerned about her daughter, particularly given her emotional state in the wake of the deaths of her father and brother, and thought the age difference was too great. In mid-November of 1942 Ruth von Wedemeyer asked Bonhoeffer not to contact her daughter for one year, given the significance of an engagement and marriage. In January 1943, however, Maria von Wedemeyer told her mother that she had decided to marry him. Her mother continued to insist that she wait, but permitted her to write. Maria von Wedemeyer wrote Bonhoeffer on January 13, 1943, that she wanted to marry him. Bonhoeffer was ecstatic:

> I can't speak otherwise than I've so often spoken in my heart in recent weeks—I want to call you what a man calls the girl with whom it is his desire and privilege to go through life, and who has given him her con-sent. Dear Maria, thank you for what you said, for all you have endured on my account, and for all you are to be and wish to be. Let us now be and become happy in each other. You must have whatever you need in the way of time and peace and quiet in which to test yourself, as you put it, just as you think fit. You alone know this. With your "yes" I, too, can now wait patiently; without that yes I was finding it hard and would have found it increasingly so. . . . I understand and have always understood in recent weeks—though not entirely without pain—that it cannot be easy for you to give me your consent, and I shall never forget that—and it's

---

28. DBWE 16:366–67.

only this "yes" of yours that can give me the courage to stop saying only "no" to myself.[29]

At the wish of her mother Bonhoeffer and Wedemeyer didn't meet in the following months; they had agreed to have no contact for six months. Bonhoeffer nonetheless wrote his fiancée on January 24, with his dangerous political activity in the background:

> You, dear Maria, have imposed a rule of silence for the next six months. It is your request, your first request for me, and what could be more natural, from my point of view, than that I should willingly grant it? I must, however, say one thing. Every self-imposed rule has its limits and dangers, and these come into play when it threatens, rather than safeguards, what is genuine and spontaneous. We have often found this to be so in years past, whenever God has overturned the plans, ideas, and ways of life we considered good and necessary. God can speak louder than our own rules. The immediate future may hold events of such elemental importance, to our private lives as well, that it would be forced and unnatural for us to be unable to communicate, if only by letter. . . .[30]

They only saw each other again in the prison.

---

29. *Love Letters from Cell 92*, 340; trans. altered.
30. Ibid., 341–42.

CHAPTER TEN

Prisoner in Tegel, 1943–1945

Locked Up

The overseas desk in the Military Intelligence office in Munich had been under observation by the Reich Central Security Office since 1942, due to suspicions of currency violations; two of the Munich office staff were arrested in the fall of 1942. Dietrich Bonhoeffer and his brother-in-law Hans von Dohnanyi took measures to cover up their conspiracy activities and contacts. In addition to falsifying his diary entries over his trips abroad, Bonhoeffer in the spring of 1943 wrote a camouflage letter to Dohnanyi, dated retroactively to November 1940, in which he offered to use his foreign contacts for "acquiring reliable information about other countries" since "leading political figures of various countries" were interested in the ecumenical movement: "This means that in fact it ought not to be difficult to ascertain the viewpoints and judgments of such figures through ecumenical relationships."[1] The Reich Central Security Office had been concerned for some time by the independence of the military secret service and wanted to put an end to this. Counselor Manfred Roeder was assigned to pursue the matter.

---

1. DBWE 16:395–96.

Dietrich Bonhoeffer in the courtyard of the Tegel military interrogation prison in Berlin in 1944

Bonhoeffer was arrested on April 5, 1943, together with Hans von Dohnanyi and his wife, Christine (Bonhoeffer's sister). Hans Oster was placed under house arrest. During Dohnanyi's imprisonment the written notes about the plans for postwar order, which implicated Bonhoeffer, were discovered.

Bonhoeffer was taken to the Tegel military interrogation prison in Berlin. Shortly afterward, he made a note of what imprisonment meant for him: "Separation—*from what is past and what is to come*."[2] His first impressions were horrifying:

> For the first night I was locked in a reception cell; the blankets on the cot stank so abominably that in spite of the cold, it was impossible to cover oneself with them. The next morning a piece of bread was thrown into my cell, so that I had to pick it up off the floor. . . . For the first time from outside my cell came the foul curses inflicted on those detained for interrogation by the prison staff; since then I have heard the abuse daily from morning till night. When I had to line up for inspection with the other new arrivals, we were addressed as "scoundrels," etc., etc. by a warder. . . . Otherwise, during the next twelve days the cell door was opened only

---

2. DBWE 8:73.

to bring me food and take out the latrine bucket. Not a single word was exchanged with me. I was given no information about why I had been imprisoned or for how long. . . . After twelve days my family connections became known in the prison.[3] For me personally this made things much easier, but it was shameful to see how everything changed from that moment on. I was moved to a more spacious cell, which an orderly cleaned for me every day. I was offered larger portions of food, which I always refused, since they would have been provided at the expense of the other prisoners; and the captain [the prison commandant] came to take me for a daily walk. The result was that the staff treated me with exceptional politeness, and some even came to apologize, saying, "Of course we didn't realize," and so on. . . . How embarrassing![4]

In the months that followed Manfred Roeder interrogated Bonhoeffer and Hans von Dohnanyi multiple times. The notes found among Dohnanyi's papers were for Roeder clear proof of his treason. Then "Operation Seven" came to light. Oster and Dohnanyi had also obtained a number of military exemptions for Confessing Church pastors, including the one for Bonhoeffer, and this raised the charge of undermining the military.

Inconsistencies in the documentation drew Roeder's attention to the date when Bonhoeffer had begun his work for the Military Counter-Intelligence. Before his assignment Bonhoeffer had apparently incorrectly stated to the Schlawe military recruitment center that he had a military assignment. For that reason, the charge filed against Bonhoeffer after six months was that he deceitfully evaded military service through an improper application for a military exemption, resulting in the charge against him of undermining the military. Roeder at that point knew nothing of Bonhoeffer and Dohnanyi's involvement in the conspiracy.

During the interrogations by Roeder, Bonhoeffer saw the necessity of protecting the ongoing coup plans as long as possible, betraying neither the plans nor those involved. This meant lying under interrogation. Bonhoeffer's essay fragment written in prison, "What does it mean to tell the truth?" attempted to address this situation theologically. For Bonhoeffer, the decisive insight was "that 'telling the truth' means different things, depending

---

3. Bonhoeffer's second cousin, Paul von Hase, was the City Commander of Berlin and hence also oversaw Tegel Prison.
4. DBWE 8:343–44.

on where one finds oneself. The relevant relationships must be taken into account. The question must be asked whether and in what way a person is justified in demanding truthful speech from another."[5] With this, Bonhoeffer negates the principled duty to state the objective facts in each and every circumstance. He offered an example: a teacher asks a child before the entire class whether it is true that his father always returns home drunk. Although this is true, the child denies it:

> In flatly saying no to the teacher's question, the response becomes untrue, to be sure; at the same time, however, it expresses the truth that the family is an order sui generis where the teacher was not justified to intrude. Of course, one could call the child's answer a lie; all the same, this lie contains more truth—i.e., it corresponds more closely to the reality—than if the child had revealed the father's weakness before the class. . . . it is the teacher alone who is guilty of the lie.[6]

Bonhoeffer did not select the example of the teacher by chance, for teachers represent a governmental-like authority. Bonhoeffer in his text is saying that his interrogator, Manfred Roeder, has no right to the truth from the conspirators. His questions are "lies." When Bonhoeffer remained silent about the facts in his answers, those answers contained "more" truth than if he had revealed the facts.

During his imprisonment Bonhoeffer also did literary work. He wrote fragments of a drama and a novel, describing the life of a middle-class family. As he told Bethge, he was trying to convey "rehabilitation of the middle class as we know it in our families, and precisely from a Christian perspective."[7] He was interested in the special behavior of the middle class in the personal and family realms, but also in its particular responsibility for establishing and maintaining a good society. He especially highlighted virtues like simplicity and the ability to remain silent. From today's perspective the literary style of the fragment appears somewhat old-fashioned. It is nonetheless interesting to see how Bonhoeffer's own experiences are woven into his portrayal, particularly which family members (under different names) appear—including Bonhoeffer himself, as well as Bethge and the von Wedemeyer family.

---

5. DBWE 16:602.
6. DBWE 16:606.
7. DBWE 8:182.

Resistance and Submission

It is no exaggeration to state that it was the correspondence with his family, Maria von Wedemeyer, and Eberhard Bethge that enabled Bonhoeffer to bear two years in prison.

At the beginning of his imprisonment Bonhoeffer could only write his family; after around four months he was then also permitted to write his fiancée. Bonhoeffer tried to ease his parents' worries, reassuring them in his first letter: "Above all you need to know and indeed believe that I am doing well."[8] He constantly expressed his gratitude toward them: "In normal life one is often not at all aware that we always receive infinitely more than we give, and that gratitude is what enriches life. One easily overestimates the importance of one's own acts and deeds, compared with what we have become only through other people."[9] He developed gratitude even for the small joys of daily prison life: "Some time ago a tit had her nest with ten young ones in a small shed here in the courtyard. I enjoyed it every day until, one day, a heartless fellow destroyed everything; some tits lay dead on the ground—incomprehensible. During my walks in the courtyard, I also enjoy a small ant hill and the bees in the linden tree."[10]

Bonhoeffer's letters to his parents reveal his attempt through self-discipline to adapt quickly to his new situation. He made out a detailed plan for the day, with set times for walking in his cell, reading, and writing. He read a great deal: the Bible, theological and other academic books, as well as literature. Through his letters he took part in family events, writing a wedding sermon for the marriage of Eberhard Bethge to Bonhoeffer's niece, Renate Schleicher, and thoughts on the baptismal day of their son, whom they named for their imprisoned friend.

In the wedding sermon Bonhoeffer describes marriage in a church as God's Yes to the Yes that the marital couple was saying to one another in love. At the same time he supports—in connection to New Testament texts but difficult to relate to in today's world—marriage as an order that needs to be preserved "since without it everything would be in disarray. In everything you are free to establish your home, but in one thing you are bound: the wife is to be subject to her husband, and the husband is to love his wife."[11] The

---

8. DBWE 8:56.
9. DBWE 8:154.
10. DBWE 8:110.
11. DBWE 8:84.

existential trauma of the dictatorship and war, and the desire for a very different kind of sphere within the world, are evident when Bonhoeffer continues: "The place to which God has assigned the wife is the home of the husband. While most people today have forgotten what a home can mean, for others of us it has become especially clear in our own time. In the midst of the world, the home is a realm of its own, a fortress amid the storms of time, a refuge, indeed, a sanctuary."[12]

Bonhoeffer also composed prayers for his fellow prisoners, taking up the situation of imprisonment: "Lord Jesus Christ, you were poor and miserable, imprisoned and abandoned as I am. You know all human need, you remain with me when no human being stands by . . ."[13] Bonhoeffer continued for some time to hope for his release.

The time together in Finkenwalde created a particularly close friendship between Bonhoeffer and Bethge—a friendship that became famous through the correspondence the two carried on during Bonhoeffer's imprisonment. They had often written each other before that period. Now the conversation with Bethge became vitally important to Bonhoeffer:

> When I read your letter yesterday, it felt like the first drops of water in a long time from a spring, in the absence of which my spiritual life had begun to wither.[14]
>
> I want you to know that, as far as possible, I'm in daily conversation with you—there's no book that I read or paragraph that I write without talking with you about it, or at least asking myself what you would say about it. In short, all of this just automatically takes the form of a letter, even when there isn't really "anything to tell."[15]

In 1951 Bethge published Bonhoeffer's letters to the family and himself under the title *Widerstand und Ergebung* (Eng.: *Resistance and Submission*); the title of the English translation is *Letters and Papers from Prison*. At the beginning he did not reveal that he was "the friend" to whom Bonhoeffer had addressed his letters. Only in 1970, with the publication of a new edition, did Bethge include excerpts from his own letters. *Letters and Papers*

---

12. DBWE 8:85.
13. DBWE 8:195.
14. DBWE 8:218.
15. DBWE 8:311.

quickly became famous. The book is a moving view of Bonhoeffer's prison experience, personal thoughts, and theological reflections. The poems that Bonhoeffer suddenly began to write in prison drew much attention, but the theological topics that had unfolded in the conversation with Bethge had the greatest impact.

Bethge's name did not initially appear in the letters to the family because the correspondence went through censors, and Bonhoeffer did not want to endanger Bethge, who knew of the conspiracy's plans. When Bethge himself was called into military service Bonhoeffer hoped that he would no longer stand under observation. At the same time, Bonhoeffer developed a friendship with a prison guard who was willing to smuggle letters to Bethge from prison, bypassing the censors. Almost seven and a half months after arriving in prison, Bonhoeffer was finally able to write his friend. He could speak to no one else as openly and was excited when he learned that Bethge would be allowed to visit him: "Tomorrow or the day after, so I am told, I will be able to talk to you. For the first time in nine months, I will be allowed to speak and hear the complete truth. That is an event. I am obliged to protect my parents and Maria; with you I will put on no pretense, nor you with me."[16]

He repeatedly gave Bethge a glimpse of his personal thoughts and feelings: "I often wonder who I really am: the one always cringing in disgust, going to pieces at these hideous experiences here, or the one who whips himself into shape, who on the outside (and even to himself) appears calm, cheerful, serene, superior, and lets himself be applauded for this charade—or is it real?"[17] He wrote that he did not regret any of the decisions that had brought him into the situation, but often asked himself "where we are to draw the line between necessary resistance [*Widerstand*] to 'fate' and equally necessary submission [*Ergebung*] . . . so my question is basically how to find the 'Thou' in this 'It' (i.e., 'fate'), or how 'fate' really becomes 'the state of being led.'"[18] Bethge chose the book title from this passage in the letters.

The theological conversations that had once more become possible with Bethge through the letters gave Bonhoeffer special pleasure. He reported how his positive assessment of the Old Testament had grown stronger in recent weeks; through this, his view of Christian hopes in the resurrection had changed:

16. DBWE 8:235.
17. DBWE 8:221.
18. DBWE 8:303–4.

I notice more and more how much I am thinking and perceiving things in line with the Old Testament; thus in recent months I have been reading much more the Old than the New Testament. Only when one knows that the name of God may not be uttered may one sometimes speak the name of Jesus Christ. Only when one loves life and the earth so much that with it everything seems to be lost and at its end may one believe in the resurrection of the dead and a new world.[19]

Despite being in prison—or perhaps because of it—this attitude toward life was a common thread throughout Bonhoeffer's letters. Bonhoeffer wasn't one to wallow in premature hopes of a better thereafter:

I believe we are so to love God in our *life* and in the good things God gives us and to lay hold of such trust in God that, when the time comes and is here—but truly only then!—we also go to God with love, trust, and joy. But—to say it clearly—that a person in the arms of his wife should long for the hereafter is, to put it mildly, tasteless and in any case is not God's will. One should find and love God in what God directly gives us; if it pleases God to allow us to enjoy an overwhelming earthly happiness, then one shouldn't be more pious than God and allow this happiness to be gnawed away through arrogant thoughts and challenges and wild religious fantasy that is never satisfied with what God gives. God will not fail the person who finds his earthly happiness in God and is grateful, in those hours when he is reminded that all earthly things are temporary and that it is good to accustom his heart to eternity, and finally the hours will not fail to come in which we can honestly say, "I wish that I were home." But all this has its time, and the main thing is that we remain in step with God and not keep rushing a few steps ahead, though also not lagging a single step behind either.[20]

Beginning with Bonhoeffer's letter to Bethge of April 30, 1944, a new stage in his theological reflections began—at least this is how he himself felt. This letter was the first in which Bonhoeffer diagnosed a "religionless age" and pondered a "non-religious interpretation" of Christian faith in this religionless

---

19. DBWE 8:213.
20. DBWE 8:228–29.

context. These were the reflections that gave *Letters and Papers* such a widespread theological reception. What was the issue here?

> What keeps gnawing at me is the question, what is Christianity, or who is Christ actually for us today? The age when we could tell people that with words—whether with theological or with pious words—is past, as is the age of inwardness and of conscience, and that means the age of religion altogether. We are approaching a completely religionless age; people as they are now simply cannot be religious anymore.[21]

To understand Bonhoeffer's analysis it must be made clear that by "religion" he wasn't referring to everything the term encompasses in our everyday usage, that is, all forms of human references to transcendence. Bonhoeffer's concept of religion was narrow and was determined by four characteristics in particular: metaphysics, inner life, individualism, and partiality. His finding was that one could no longer believe in this way. Metaphysics had determined God as the highest, omnipotent, world-removed being that serves as an explanation when human beings are unable to explain certain realities within the world, and which intervenes in the world from outside, when human beings stumble on their limitations and no longer know how to help themselves. When the religious, metaphysical God is located in human limitations, it is in religion's interest to strengthen the boundaries of human beings—not just their epistemological boundaries but also their interior boundaries where they don't know how to go on, their inner life. The religious thesis is that only with God can human beings cope with their questions arising at these boundaries, with the so-called ultimate questions about suffering, guilt, and death. This, however, renders religion essentially something oriented toward individualism— that is, the personal concerns of individuals for their inner well-being and the salvation of their souls. All three characteristics—metaphysics, inner life, and individualism—have the common feature that through them religion becomes something partial, something that affects only a part of human life but never the human being in his or her entirety.

Bonhoeffer observed that these four characteristics do not describe an anthropological constant that is some kind of necessary need in human beings, but a historically determined and transitory human expression. In the last

---

21. DBWE 8:362.

centuries human beings had "come of age" and could now live without that kind of divine guardian at the boundaries of their knowledge and inner life:

> The movement toward human autonomy (by which I mean discovery of the laws by which the world lives and manages its affairs in science, in society and government, in art, ethics, and religion), which began around the thirteenth century (I don't want to get involved in disputing exactly when), has reached a certain completeness in our age. The human being has learned to manage all important issues by himself, without recourse to "Working hypothesis: God." . . . it's becoming evident that everything gets along without "God" and does so just as well as before.[22]

"As a working hypothesis for morality, politics, and the natural sciences, God has been overcome and done away with," in the realm of knowledge as in the realm of human behavior.[23] This was "also true of the universal human questions": "Today, even for these questions, there are human answers that can completely disregard God. Human beings cope with these questions practically without God and have done so throughout the ages."[24]

In Bonhoeffer's appraisal, the church had fought this development for too long. It had demonized worldly explanations that were independent of God, such as Darwinism, and attempted "to prove to secure, contented, and happy human beings that they are in reality miserable and desperate and just don't want to admit that they are in a perilous situation, unbeknown to themselves."[25] Later, he wrote,

> Religious people speak of God at a point where human knowledge is at an end (or sometimes when they're too lazy to think further), or when human strength fails. Actually, it's a *deus ex machina* that they're always bringing on the scene, either to appear to solve insoluble problems or to provide strength when human powers fail, thus always exploiting human weakness or human limitations. Inevitably that lasts only until human beings become powerful enough to push the boundaries a bit further and God is no longer needed as *deus ex machina*.[26]

---

22. DBWE 8:425–26.
23. DBWE 8:478.
24. DBWE 8:406.
25. DBWE 8:427.
26. DBWE 8:366.

God is always "smuggled in somewhere" by the church, "in the very last, secret place that is left,"[27] instead of the church acknowledging the maturity of human beings and their religionlessness.

Such a recognition was not a resigned accommodation to realities, but a consequence of that which, in Bonhoeffer's view, had already taken place in Jesus Christ's death on the cross. The God on the cross contradicted the metaphysical notion of an omnipotent God, for Christ on the cross was marked by powerlessness and suffering. God himself suffered pain, isolation, and the forsakenness of God on the cross (cf. Mark 15:34). This powerless, suffering, godforsaken God on the cross is "the opposite of everything a religious person expects from God."[28]

Yet, through God's suffering, the suffering and godforsakenness of every human being is changed; from this point on they have their place next to and in God. Whoever suffers, whoever feels forsaken by God, is not separated from God. It is much more the case that God already meets that person. Moreover, the powerless God illustrates that human beings cannot find refuge in a God that intervenes in the world from outside. When God allows Godself to be pushed out of the world, God affirms the world come of age. Human beings can and must come to terms with their own lives independently—and know at the same time "that God is near and present with us":[29]

> . . . we cannot be honest unless we recognize that we have to live in the world—"*etsi deus non daretur.*" And this is precisely what we do recognize—before God! God himself compels us to recognize it. Thus our coming of age leads us to a truer recognition of our situation before God. God would have us know that we must live as those who manage their lives without God. The same God who is with us is the God who forsakes us (Mark 15:34!). The same God who makes us to live in the world without the working hypothesis of God is the God before whom we stand continually. Before God, and with God, we live without God.[30]

The goal of this perspective on modern humanity that has been won from the cross is a new worldliness, in which Christians turn to this world with courage

---

27. DBWE 8:457.
28. DBWE 8:480.
29. DBWE 8:515.
30. DBWE 8:478–79.

and openness. They should no longer orbit fearfully around themselves, but be there for others. "The church is church only when it is there for others."[31] This occurs when human beings participate in the suffering of this world and the suffering of God because of and in the world.

Against the backdrop of these fundamental reflections, Bonhoeffer demanded a "non-religious interpretation of biblical concepts,"[32] in which Christianity is rethought. Although it has often been understood otherwise, Bonhoeffer did not mean by this that Christianity should relinquish its faith in God, that people should give up religious practices like prayer and ritual, or that there should no longer be a church. No, all these things are part of Christianity. But Christianity should orient itself so that God, faith, and church are conceived without the religious elements listed above, so that they exist for the good of the world. Bonhoeffer was able only to touch in the letters on what such an interpretation would look like. He began to write a short monograph about it, but was unable to complete it, and it has not been preserved.

On July 20, 1944, the assassination attempt carried out by Claus Schenk Graf von Stauffenberg failed. In its wake, Dietrich Bonhoeffer's brother Klaus and brother-in-law Rüdiger Schleicher were arrested, like many others, and murdered on April 23, 1945, in Moabit Prison. Bonhoeffer's knowledge of the failed assassination attempt is evident in his letter to Bethge of July 21, 1944, in which he wrote that the decisive question was not what would come of himself but, rather, that one could live responsibly in the world:

> I discovered, and am still discovering to this day, that one only learns to have faith by living in the full this-worldliness of life. If one has completely renounced making something of oneself—whether it be a saint or a converted sinner or a church leader (a so-called priestly figure!), a just or an unjust person, a sick or a healthy person—then one throws oneself completely into the arms of God, and this is what I call this-worldliness: living fully in the midst of life's tasks, questions, successes and failures, experiences, and perplexities—then one takes seriously no longer one's own sufferings but rather the suffering of God in the world. Then one stays awake with Christ in Gethsemane. And I think this is faith; this is *metanoia*. And this is how one becomes a human being, a Christian.[33]

---

31. DBWE 8:503.
32. DBWE 8:475.
33. DBWE 8:486.

Love Letters from Cell 92

In the early period of Bonhoeffer's imprisonment he was only allowed to write his parents, so Maria von Wedemeyer only received indirect messages from her fiancé. She wrote letters to him that she didn't send, as, for example, one month after his arrest:

> I doubt if there's an hour in the day when my thoughts don't turn to you. When I walk through the garden at 6 A.M., on my way to the hospital, I know that you're awake too, and that you may even be looking up at the same sky. While I'm dressing the four little children . . . in my care, I tell them lots of long stories about "Uncle Dietrich." When I'm scrubbing and polishing, I think "Dietrich, Dietrich" in time to my movements. And when I discuss first names with my women's ward, you can be sure they all agree that "Dietrich" is the nicest. I hold your picture in my hand every night and tell you lots of things—lots of "do you remembers" and "later ons"—so many of them that I finally can't help believing that

Eberhard Bethge and Dietrich Bonhoeffer in front of the parsonage in Groß-Schlönwitz in 1938

they're only a *small* step away from the present. And then I tell you all the things that can't be put into writing—certainly not if other people have to read my letters—but things you already know without my writing them down.[34]

After the separation demanded by her mother, they saw each other again for the first time on June 24, 1943, under the eyes of Manfred Roeder. A short time later Bonhoeffer was permitted to write her. Their letters to one another, included in the 1992 book *Love Letters from Cell 92*,[35] are full of love and affection. They reassured each other that there was no need to worry, borne by their hopes for a future together. Bonhoeffer wrote her:

> You can't possibility imagine what it means to me, in my present predicament, to have you. I'm under God's special guidance here, I feel sure. To me, the way in which we found each other such a short time before my arrest seems a definite indication of that. Once again, things went "*hominum confusione et dei providentia*" ("according to man's confusion and God's providence"). It amazes me anew every day how little I have deserved such happiness, just as it daily and deeply moves me that God should have put you through such an ordeal this past year, and that he so clearly meant me to bring you grief and sorrow, so soon after we got to know each other, to endow our love with the proper foundation and the proper strength. Moreover, when I consider the state of the world, the total obscurity enshrouding our personal destiny, and my present imprisonment, our union—if it wasn't frivolity, which it certainly wasn't—can only be a token of God's grace and goodness, which summon us to believe in him. . . . When Jeremiah said, in his people's hour of direst need, that "houses and fields (and vineyards) shall again be brought in this land" (Jer. 32:15), it was a token of confidence in the future. That requires faith, and may God grant it to us daily. I don't mean the faith that flees the world, but the faith that endures *in* the world and loves and remains true to that world in spite of all the hardships it brings us. Our marriage must be a "yes" to God's earth. It must strengthen our resolve to do and

---

34. Ruth-Alice von Bismarck and Ulrich Kabitz, eds., *Love Letters from Cell 92: The Correspondence between Dietrich Bonhoeffer and Maria von Wedemeyer*, trans. John Brownjohn (Nashville: Abingdon, 1995), 23.
35. The U.S. edition was published in 1995.

accomplish something on earth. I fear that Christians who venture to stand on earth on only one leg will stand in heaven on only one leg too.[36]

For both of them, the relationship was fed by their trust in God. But it wasn't so much the theological questions they discussed in their letters, even if she was trying to learn more about Bonhoeffer's thought: "At nights I always dip into your books. A lot of things escape me, and I look forward to asking you about them."[37] She wrote much about her daily life and was already planning what they needed for their future household. He sent her recommendations for books she should read, because he found her literary tastes unsuitable. The letters also reveal how greatly they both suffered under the separation and their uncertain future. On January 13, 1944, the anniversary of their engagement, she wrote him: "You mustn't think you have to make up for anything. You're not to write like that. It only hurts. The pain isn't mine at all, it's yours, and you give me a share of your pain to bear. I'm grateful for it—in fact I actually welcome it because we're able to bear it together. We have so few things in common."[38] Bonhoeffer revealed to Bethge, however, his insecurity about the relationship, above all because Bonhoeffer and Wedemeyer did not yet know one another that well and because, for Bonhoeffer, love "can only grow from knowing the other person fully, or at least from intense togetherness with her."[39] He was certain that this would develop with her, but he noted such an intensity in her letters to him that he worried he was being less than open to her.

She was able on occasion to visit Bonhoeffer. After one such visit in June 1944 he sent her the poem "The Past":

You left, beloved bliss and pain so hard to love.
What shall I call you? Life, Anguish, Ecstasy,
my Heart, of my own self a part—the past?
The door slammed shut and locked,
I hear your steps depart, resound, then slowly fade.
What remains for me? Joy, torment, longing?
I know just this: You left—and all is past.
Do you feel how I reach for you now,

---

36. Ibid., 63–64.
37. Ibid., 30.
38. Ibid., 158–59.
39. DBWE 8:277.

how I clutch you as with claws,
so tightly that it must hurt?
How I wound your flesh
till your blood oozes out,
just to be assured you are near,
you bodily, earthly fullness of life?
Do you sense my terrible longing for pain of my own?
that I yearn to see my own blood
just so that all will not fade away
into the past?

. . .

I stretch out my hands
and pray—
and I discover:
Your life's most vital piece may be
the past, a gift you may regain
through gratitude and rueful pain.
Grasp God's forgiveness and goodness in the past,
pray that God keep you this day and to the last.[40]

The verses that Bonhoeffer sent to Wedemeyer at the end of 1944 would become famous. He was now in a basement cell of the prison on the Prinz-Albrecht-Strasse. In his letter accompanying the poem he wrote:

I haven't for an instant felt lonely and forlorn. You yourself, my parents—all of you including my friends and students on active service—are my constant companions. Your prayers and kind thoughts, passages from the Bible, long-forgotten conversations, pieces of music, books—all are invested with life and reality as never before. I live in a great, unseen realm of whose real existence I'm in no doubt.[41]

The poem he wrote for her, "The Powers of Good," described this reality, sent as a "Christmas greeting" to Wedemeyer and his family. Only when one knows the circumstances under which it was written can the somber tone that underlies his confidence and trust be heard:

---

40. DBWE 8:418–19, 421.
41. *Love Letters from Cell 92*, 268–69.

1. By faithful, quiet powers of good surrounded
so wondrously consoled and sheltered here—
I wish to live these days with you in spirit
and with you enter into a new year.

2. The old year still would try our hearts to torment,
of evil times we still do bear the weight;
O Lord, do grant our souls, now terror-stricken,
salvation for which you did us create.

3. And should you offer us the cup of suffering,
though heavy, brimming full and bitter brand,
we'll thankfully accept it, never flinching,
from your good heart and your beloved hand.

4. But should you wish now once again to give us
the joys of this world and its glorious sun,
then we'll recall anew what past times brought us
and then our life belongs to you alone.

5. The candles you have brought into our darkness,
let them today be burning warm and bright,
and if it's possible, do reunite us!
We know your light is shining through the night.

6. When now the quiet deepens all around us,
O, let our ears that fullest sound amaze
of this, your world, invisibly expanding
as all your children sing high hymns of praise.

7. By powers of good so wondrously protected,
we wait with confidence, befall what may.
God is with us at night and in the morning
and oh, most certainly on each new day.[42]

---

42. DBWE 8:548–50.

The Final Months

After the Gestapo's discovery of the resistance group's secret archive in Zossen on September 22, 1944, Bonhoeffer could no longer hope to be released, since the files implicated him in the July 20 conspiracy plans. After a guard offered to help him, he briefly considered escaping from prison. Yet in light of his brother Klaus's arrest on October 1, Bonhoeffer decided against it, fearing that his escape would endanger his family as well as his fiancée.

On October 8, 1944, Bonhoeffer was moved to the underground prison of the Reich Central Security Headquarters on Prinz-Albrecht-Strasse. He was in an adjoining cell to Fabian von Schlabrendorff (who was Maria von Wedemeyer's cousin). Admiral Canaris, General Oster, and Carl Goerdeler were also imprisoned there, and his brother-in-law Hans von Dohnanyi was moved there from Sachsenhausen in late January 1945. Bonhoeffer was able to write only three more letters. There were new interrogations.

On February 3, 1945, a major air raid on Berlin destroyed the Reich Central Security Headquarters. Bonhoeffer and nineteen other prominent prisoners were moved on February 7 to the Buchenwald concentration camp. On April 3 the group was transported to Schönberg, Bavaria. A survivor reported later that Bonhoeffer held morning devotions for his fellow prisoners on April 7. He was then separated from the group and taken to the Flossenbürg concentration camp. British fellow prisoner Payne Best later reported that before Bonhoeffer was taken away he gave Best a message for George Bell, repeating it to him twice with emphasis, making Best wonder whether Bonhoeffer's words were a coded message for Bell—an interpretation that Bell subsequently denied:

> Will you give this message from me to the Bishop of Chichester, "tell him that this is for me the end, but also the beginning—with him I believe in the principle of our Universal Christian brotherhood which rises above all national hatreds and that our victory is certain—tell him, too, that I have never forgotten his words at our last meeting.[43]

Dietrich Bonhoeffer was summarily sentenced to death in a mock trial on April 8. On April 9, 1945, only one month before the end of the war, he was hanged to death, together with Wilhelm Canaris, Ludwig Gehre, Hans Oster, Karl Sack, and Theodor Strünck.

---

43. DBWE 16:468–69.

A MODERN SAINT?

The Reception of Bonhoeffer after 1945

The widespread renown and respect for Dietrich Bonhoeffer is due primarily to his consistent, courageous life during the Nazi dictatorship and his early, violent death. His murder by the Nazis seems to confirm the rightness of his life. For many people, Bonhoeffer has become a memorial to what responsible action during the National Socialist era should have looked like. At the same time, he is also cherished as a model of credible Christian life today.

When one observes the reception of Bonhoeffer it is immediately striking to see how strongly people from very different theological backgrounds and sectors in the Christian world have adopted him for their own purposes. Critics of the institutional church refer to him, as do institutional church representatives. Liberal theologians quote him, as do conservative groups. Those taking their various positions usually draw on very different Bonhoeffer texts. Liberation theologians resonate primarily with the prison writings, while more pietistic groups draw on *Discipleship* and other texts from the Finkenwalde period. Isolated Bonhoeffer sentences are torn from their theological and historical context, and people assume that the truths he spoke to the challenges of his era can be applied to various contemporary issues. People naively ask: "What would Bonhoeffer say?"

People draw on Bonhoeffer to testify to very different positions, first, because of the theological scope of his work. Another reason is the fragmentary nature of many of his writings: Bonhoeffer only published about one fifth of his writings himself. He was unable to complete many texts, which leaves them open to very different interpretations. The third reason for the instrumentalization of Bonhoeffer has already been named: his unusual and exemplary life and his premature death.

Interest in Bonhoeffer's life and thought began shortly after his death not in Germany, but abroad, driven largely by his ecumenical friends. On July 27, 1945, Bishop George Bell and Bonhoeffer's friends Franz Hildebrandt and Julius Rieger held a memorial church service for him in London. By the end of 1945 the World Council of Churches, in the process of formation, had published a memorial booklet under the direction of Willem Visser 't Hooft, titled *Das Zeugnis eines Boten* ("Testimony of a Messenger"). There, some of Bonhoeffer's prison writings were published for the first time. Both this and the London memorial service honored Bonhoeffer as a witness to Jesus Christ and a martyr, while postwar Germans had more difficulties using such words for Bonhoeffer. With the passage of time, however, people in Germany began to take greater note of him. On the first anniversary of his death, April 9, 1946, Eberhard Bethge published Bonhoeffer's poems from Tegel prison for the first time, under the title *Auf dem Wege zur Freiheit* ("On the Way to Freedom"). In general, however, serious study of Bonhoeffer in Germany began years later.

Thus, the postwar reception of Bonhoeffer began not with academic examination of his theology, but with respect and fascination for his life and person. It included accounts such as that of the doctor who worked at the Flossenbürg concentration camp and was present at Bonhoeffer's execution. He reported that Bonhoeffer had bravely climbed the steps to the gallows and died after a few seconds, with complete and unshakeable trust in God. In the meantime, it has become clear that this story was concocted by the doctor and sugarcoated the actual event.

In the early postwar period in Germany many people had great difficulties with Bonhoeffer's political resistance, including the conspiracy's violence. His behavior was questioned in light of the Christian duty "to be subservient to authority." Wasn't it a Christian duty to be obedient to the state, since the state's authority came from God? Was Bonhoeffer's participation in the resistance an act of responsibility or treason? During this period his decisions were criticized like those of the other July 20 resistance figures. From a theological perspective, his behavior in the conspiracy seemed to conflict with his exhortations to peace during the 1930s, and it seemed as if he had abandoned his emphasis on peace through his support for the coup attempt. This led some to conclude that Bonhoeffer in his last years was no longer acting on the basis of Christian ethics, and that only his involvement in the Confessing Church could be honored as Christian.

Yet there were also other voices. More than anyone else, Eberhard Bethge interpreted Bonhoeffer's participation in the resistance as an immediate expression of his Christian faith. Others stressed that violent resistance within certain parameters might even have been conceivable for Martin Luther. Gradually, the assessment of the July 20 conspirators began to change, and with that the judgments about Bonhoeffer's political engagement as well.

In the course of the 1950s, scholarly interest in Bonhoeffer began to grow, provoked primarily by Bethge's 1951 German edition of *Letters and Papers from Prison*. Many enthusiastically took Bonhoeffer's fragmentary sketches about the world come of age and the necessity of a "nonreligious" Christianity as liberating and trailblazing. In a society in which fewer people considered themselves to be religious, Bonhoeffer's theses made Christian faith still relevant and vital. His demand for a different, liberating language and a new interpretation of classical Christian themes freed people for a way of being Christian that took modern people seriously in their worldliness and independence.

The appearance of *Letters and Papers from Prison* awakened an interest among many readers in Bonhoeffer's other theological works. Thus, the scholarly interest in Bonhoeffer started with the end, so to speak. His *Ethics* became interesting as preparation for his prison theology. *Discipleship* and *Life Together* were interpreted in terms of the tensions with his later reflections and, to some extent, as a retreat from the world, a position from which some scholars believed that Bonhoeffer had freed himself in his later writings. Finally, his early academic works were analyzed in the search for the basic motives that reappeared in his later works.

Only in more recent years have scholars become aware of how reading Bonhoeffer from the end to the beginning can distort one's interpretation of him. People claim to discover certain concepts in his early writings that do not in fact exist there. The early and middle writings of Bonhoeffer are now more strongly appreciated in their own right, and less as preparations for his later work.

Two major works were fundamental for the recognition of Bonhoeffer's life and theology: the monumental biography by Eberhard Bethge, which was published in 1967 in Germany[1] and which still is the definitive work on Bonhoeffer's life; it was followed in 1971 by Catholic theologian Ernst Feil's dissertation, *Die Theologie Dietrich Bonhoeffers: Hermeneutik—Christologie—Weltverständnis.*[2]

Bethge remains the most important interpreter of Bonhoeffer; without him Bonhoeffer would not have become as well known. With the biography and the edition of Bonhoeffer's unpublished writings, as well as his numerous lectures in Germany and abroad, Bethge shaped the portrait of Bonhoeffer for those who had not known him. In his work Bethge divided Bonhoeffer's life into three phases: the period as an academic theologian (until 1931); that of the steadfast Christian (until 1940); and that of the critical "man for his times" (after 1940).

For a long time Bonhoeffer scholars debated about whether each new phase really represented a turn away from the previous one, or whether—as some interpreters thought—the late Bonhoeffer was the "true Bonhoeffer." In particular, the question was hotly debated about where to locate the "middle-phase Bonhoeffer" of the Finkenwalde years. In recent years, the perspective has been more that, while Bonhoeffer over the course of his life reacted to new personal, theological, and sociopolitical challenges, he held fast to his basic decisions. These included the strong orientation to Jesus Christ and the church, as well as the search for a Christian existence that encompassed human action.

Ernst Feil's portrayal of Bonhoeffer's theology went through several printings and is still in print today; it illustrates a peculiar aspect of Bonhoeffer's reception: the appreciation he found among Catholic theologians. There are few other twentieth-century Protestant theologians who have been considered as much in Catholic monographs and studies.

Among Protestants, Bonhoeffer played an important role in the church positions on political issues in the Federal Republic of Germany and the German Democratic Republic. He became the symbol of the Christian obligation

---

1. The first English translation appeared in 1970.
2. An English translation was published as *The Theology of Dietrich Bonhoeffer*, trans. Martin Rumscheidt (Philadelphia: Fortress Press, 1985).

to become politically engaged. His early awareness of political evils, such as the National Socialist policies against the Jews, was a model. During the peace movement of the 1980s Bonhoeffer's pacifist statements were recalled. His ideal of a peace council of churches, which he had formulated at the 1934 Fanø meeting, was taken up by the 1985 German Protestant Kirchentag (a national lay church convention) and became an important precedent for the ecumenical Conciliar Process of the Churches for Justice, Peace, and the Integrity of Creation.

During the Cold War era, Bonhoeffer became even more of a Christian model in the German Democratic Republic (East Germany) than in the western Federal Republic. The attempt to read his "nonreligious" interpretation of Christian faith as an encouragement for the church in a socialist society was as prominent as it was controversial. In the German Democratic Republic, too, the church had to take its responsibility to be "the church for others" seriously, and the slogan "the church in socialism" could be traced to this perspective of Bonhoeffer's. It was, however, interpreted in different ways. Did it mean the church's acceptance of the socialist reality, or critical involvement for the sake of what East German theologian Heino Falcke called "a socialism that could be improved"? In the other Communist countries of eastern Europe, too, Bonhoeffer stimulated thoughts about how the church could live without privilege in a secular society.

There were numerous academic works on Bonhoeffer in the German Democratic Republic, including ideological works that used his thought to defend existing socialism. One of these works was the first general study of Bonhoeffer's theology, written by Berlin theologian Hanfried Müller, whose book *Von der Kirche zur Welt* ("From the Church to the World") appeared in 1961. Müller considered Bonhoeffer's late theology to be the foundation for a comprehensive affirmation of atheistic Marxism among Christians. In the wake of such interpretation, the German Democratic Republic adopted Bonhoeffer as an "anti-fascist resistance fighter." The Christian Democratic Union party in the east touted the German Democratic Republic as the future for which Bonhoeffer had been fighting. Bonhoeffer was also adopted by the other side, however, as an exemplar: many opposition figures were inspired by him to their resistance against the injustices of the socialist state—for that reason, Bonhoeffer's *Ethics* was never published in the German Democratic Republic.

No other twentieth-century German theologian has an international audience like Bonhoeffer, not only among academics but among pastors, religious educators, and lay Christians as well. His books have been translated into numerous languages. The International Bonhoeffer Society, founded in 1971, has sections in many countries to maintain Bonhoeffer's academic and church legacy and help it bear fruit in the contemporary world.

In the English-speaking world, Bonhoeffer's adoption during the 1960s as a "God is dead" theologian sparked a furor. Proponents of this theology, which rejects a personal or otherworldly God, took up many of Bonhoeffer's phrases, such as his statement that the person come of age lives "before God, and with God . . . without God."[3] In the "death of God" movement's departure from theism, central fundamental elements of Christian faith were transformed or even rejected with the aim of developing a new, secular faith. With that, however, they took Bonhoeffer's late theology in abbreviated form, confusing his concept of "worldly Christianity" with secularism.

Bonhoeffer's theology has also been fruitful for North American black theology and African American liberation theology. Bonhoeffer has been adopted as a model by some of these theologians because of the existential rootedness of his theology and his consequent action. Bonhoeffer also offers impulses for other trajectories of North and Latin American liberation theology. In addition, both conservative and liberal politicians holding very different sentiments have adopted him. At the same time, there have been numerous research works in the United States on Bonhoeffer's theology that, in contrast to German works, use his thought as the foundation for new individual or social ethical concepts.

The fascination with Bonhoeffer in the United States continues, with completely contrasting portrayals of Bonhoeffer. Liberals since the 1960s have claimed him as the symbol of a critical patriotism and quote him in their critiques of U.S. foreign policy, particularly with respect to issues of militarism. In contrast, conservatives honor Bonhoeffer as an exemplary Christian who lived a life of personal discipleship and struggled honorably against the evils of the world. In addition, people like to take Bonhoeffer's critique of his own church for their criticisms of contemporary U.S. Christianity.

Bonhoeffer has been particularly inspiring for opposition groups in non-democratic countries who have explored resistance against oppression. In 1973 Eberhard Bethge took a lecture tour of South Africa; after that, Bonhoeffer's theology played a significant role in the political struggles there. His fearless life became a model in the struggle against apartheid. Like Bonhoeffer, many

---

3. DBWE 8:479.

South African Christians sought to "seize the wheel itself,"[4] and felt that his work empowered the church there to play a role in the political questions. Bonhoeffer's fight against antisemitic policies was applied to the issue of racial discrimination there. The South African church could not allow itself to support such discrimination or give it theological legitimacy. After the first democratic elections in South Africa in 1994, Bonhoeffer's demand for the church's confession of guilt in light of its failure under National Socialism[5] was applied to the church situation in South Africa, for without a church confession of guilt there could be no reconciliation.

Bonhoeffer's life and work played a particular role in Asia, where Christians are a minority. In Japan the involvement with Bonhoeffer led to strong self-criticism, since people there recognized that Christians should have resisted the nationalistic, totalitarian state Shintoism. In South Korea, Christians fighting the military dictatorships of the 1960s and 1970s drew on Bonhoeffer's political resistance. The story of his life encouraged people to resist and his demand for a kind of Christianity in this world that didn't evade suffering helped people to endure their own suffering. Bonhoeffer's thought was incorporated into Korean Minjung theology, which fought for justice, human rights, and democracy.

Besides such political motives, there is an entirely different reason for Bonhoeffer's worldwide appeal: the moving passages from his writings, especially his poems, which have found their way into gift books, posters, and postcards. One doesn't need to read an entire book to be inspired by his thoughts. Bonhoeffer has found his way into other media: oratoria and stage plays, novels, movies and documentary films, paintings and sculptures. His influence is found far beyond the realm of academic theology—so that sometimes the academic focus on him is even suspected of serving other, nonacademic goals.

In the meantime, Bonhoeffer's reception itself has become a topic of academic study. Almost all his contemporaries and the first generation of Bonhoeffer scholars are gone, and the second generation has now retired. For younger scholars the Third Reich is in the distant past. They are able to regard Bonhoeffer's writings uninfluenced by the early debates and free of the personal and family ties that some of the earlier scholars had. This historicization brings with it a more critical view of Bonhoeffer that is shaped by the moral and social positions of today. His statements about gender roles, for example,

---

4. DBWE 12:365.
5. DBWE 16:572ff.

or his conservative political positions are criticized. His role in the rescue of Jews and his involvement in political resistance are seen more soberly, and the earlier emphasis on the uniqueness of his role has been challenged. The portrait of a lone righteous prophet in the desert has faded. Scholars today increasingly follow Eberhard Jüngel's 1982 demand: "Because of the course of his life and his violent end, a nimbus of theological unassailability has risen around Bonhoeffer's work, but it has done damage. One should destroy this nimbus for Bonhoeffer's sake."[6]

Dietrich Bonhoeffer Today

Although many of Bonhoeffer's writings continue to speak to readers today, it cannot be forgotten that they were written many decades ago. Bonhoeffer's insights address a very different social, political, and intellectual situation and cannot simply be applied to today. We no longer share many of Bonhoeffer's views, including his conservative Prussian political worldview and his very traditional understanding of family.

Nor, however, can one simply adopt the positions that appear to be contemporary. Many of his decisions that we view today as good, correct, and self-evident were, in the situation of his times, anything but clear. His radicality and refusal to compromise, which was what his particular political situation demanded, cannot simply be adopted for today. Nonetheless, it is worthwhile at the end of this book to go beyond the historical and reflect on the contemporary relevance of Bonhoeffer's thought. This can only mean taking note of the impulses that can stimulate our own thoughts and judgments about our very different situation today.

First, Bonhoeffer remains interesting as a person who tried to preserve the relationship between faith, theology, and life. Faith and theology, for him, were not private or academic mental games; they had existential significance and immediate effects on action. The reverse was also true: Bonhoeffer constantly allowed his own faith and theology to be challenged by the circumstances of his life. He reexamined his own ideas and convictions when they no longer seemed suited for new situations. It was more important to him that his thought corresponded to reality than that he maintain some theological system. One can learn much from Bonhoeffer's capacity to start over again

---

6. Eberhard Jüngel, "Das Geheimnis der Stellvertretung," in *Wertlose Wahrheit: zur Identität und Relevanz des christlichen Glaubens* (Munich: Chr. Kaiser Verlag, 1990), 253.

"from the very beginning," wrestling with his own faith and theology, and the willingness to retest the ideas to which one has become accustomed. It was not a matter of dismissing the Christian tradition, but of reexamining its significance for the present. This was the perspective articulated in Bonhoeffer's central question: "What is Christianity, or who is Christ actually for us today?"[7]

Bonhoeffer's orientation toward Christ always went together with his conviction that Christian community, the church, is necessary for Christian life. One cannot be a Christian for oneself alone but, rather, only together with others. In recent decades this insight has not always been respected in Protestantism. One often hears that the particular mark of Protestant Christian life—in contrast to Catholicism—is that one can believe without the church. This overlooks the fact, however, that Christians are already bound with one another through their faith in Christ. They already constitute a fellowship through Christ, whether they are conscious of this or not, or as Bonhoeffer stated, "Christian community means community through Jesus Christ and in Jesus Christ."[8] Moreover, the individual Christian needs other Christians, for no one can speak the central Christian message of the unconditional love of God to oneself. This message cannot be discovered in one's own self-judgment; it must be spoken by other human beings. Even today, then, Bonhoeffer's warning deserves a hearing: "Christians need other Christians who speak God's Word to them. They need them again and again when they become uncertain and disheartened. . . ."[9]

The church is not only a place for personal Christian existence, however; it has a particular social and political function. Although Bonhoeffer lived in a different church-state situation than we do today, there is still contemporary meaning to his challenge that the church must "be there for others" and remind the state of its duty to care for justice, order (and peace). In this the church may not think it is the better politician. Good policy requires political competency, detailed knowledge, and training in the ability to judge—abilities that do not automatically come with Christian faith. But while politics always runs the risk of losing itself in the details of the politics of the day or, in the worst case, loses its sense of its purpose, the church has an eye for the things for whose sake the state exists. Because its primary task stands outside the political realities, the church is able to remind the state of its own task. The

---

7. DBWE 8:362.
8. DBWE 5:31.
9. DBWE 5:32.

church should "keep asking the government whether its actions can be justified as *legitimate state* actions, that is, actions that create law and order, not lack of rights and disorder. . . . This does not mean interfering in the state's responsibility for its actions; on the contrary, it is thrusting the entire burden of responsibility upon the state itself for the actions proper to it."[10] In general, these suggestions of Bonhoeffer lean in the direction of what more recently has been described as "public theology."

Bonhoeffer's relevance has also been disputed in recent years. Given what sociologists and theologians observe as the revival of religion, Bonhoeffer's thesis that we are approaching a "religionless age" in which people wish to live without religion does not seem to have become true. Yet, particularly in such a situation, Bonhoeffer's demand for a "nonreligious interpretation" of the Christian message has importance—if his analysis is correct that "religion" (if understood in the manner described above) does not correspond to the essence of Christian faith. Bonhoeffer reminds us that religion is not meant to develop at the cost of the world and the dismissal of the worldly. It is not meant to offer people a retreat from the world but, rather, to help us live responsibly in this world. Yet Bonhoeffer was just as opposed to the antireligious view that faith is bad for modern human beings and their world as he was to the kind of religion that rejects the world. His argument was that it is possible to believe in such a way that faith in God, modern autonomy, and responsibility to the world do not rule each other out. A human being can be at the same time intellectually of age, ethically autonomous, and believe in God.

Globalization and new technical possibilities, especially in the medical and biotechnological spheres, have rendered the ethical decisions that we face increasingly complex, more difficult, and with wider consequences. In light of all the new ethical questions arising, an ethic based purely on principles— where we may think we know where the norm lies that holds true for all questions, even those that have not yet been asked—meets its limits. Yet, an ethics of conviction that shies away from making hard decisions that are overshadowed by ambivalence also threatens to make us incapable of action. Finally, an "ethic of goods" (*Güterethik*), which has as its criterion the goods that should be achieved through ethical behavior, fails when the consequences of our own actions are unpredictable. Bonhoeffer's approach with an ethics of responsibility does not resolve all these dilemmas, but it encourages us to a sober analysis of the given situation and a courageous response to the needs of the other

10. DBWE 12:364.

person who encounters us concretely, borne by the hope in God's forgiveness of the responsible act.

> No one has the responsibility of turning the world into the kingdom of God. . . . Responsibility is limited both in its scope and in its character, i.e., both quantitatively and qualitatively. . . . The task is not to turn the world upside down but in a given place to do what, from the perspective of reality, is necessary objectively and to really carry it out.[11]

---

11. DBWE 6:224–25.

CHRONOLOGY

1906

February 4   Dietrich Bonhoeffer and his twin sister Sabine born in Breslau

1912

Spring   Bonhoeffer family moves to Berlin, where Karl Bonhoeffer takes position at the Berlin Charité Hospital

1918

April 28   Dietrich's older brother Walter is killed in the First World War

1923

March 1   Dietrich Bonhoeffer takes his secondary school examinations

Summer   Bonhoeffer begins his theological studies in Tübingen

1924

April–June	Bonhoeffer and his brother Klaus travel to Italy and North Africa. In June Bonhoeffer continues his theological studies in Berlin

1927

December 17	Bonhoeffer receives his doctorate *summa cum laude* under Reinhold Seeberg for his dissertation *Sanctorum Communio* (published in 1930)

1928

January 17	Bonhoeffer passes his first theological examinations toward ordination
February	Beginning of Bonhoeffer's foreign assistantship (i.e., period as vicar) in a German congregation in Barcelona

1929

February	Return to Germany
Summer semester	Bonhoeffer takes an assistantship under Wilhelm Lütgert and begins work on his postdoctoral dissertation

1930

July 8	Bonhoeffer passes his second theological examinations toward ordination
July 18	Habilitation in Systematic Theology with the postdoctoral dissertation *Act and Being: Transcendental Philosophy and Ontology in Systematic Theology* (published in German in 1931)
After September	Study year at Union Theological Seminary in New York City

1931

June	Return from the United States
July	Three-week visit with Karl Barth in Bonn
After August	Assistantship under Wilhelm Lütgert
September 1–5	Participation in the meeting of the World Alliance for Promoting International Friendship through the Churches; Bonhoeffer elected as one of three youth secretaries
November 2	Bonhoeffer begins his duties as a lecturer at University of Berlin
November 15	Bonhoeffer ordained in St. Matthew's Church in Berlin. He becomes the student chaplain at the Technical College in Charlottenburg, and gives confirmation classes at Zion church in central Berlin

1932

March 19–29	Confirmation retreat in Friedrichsbrunn
July 20–30	Participation in the Youth Peace Conference of the World Alliance in Ciernohorské Kúpele, Czechoslovakia
August 25–31	Participation in the Youth Conference of the World Alliance and the Ecumenical Council for Life and Work in Gland, Switzerland
Winter semester	Lectures at University of Berlin on "Creation and Sin" (published in 1933 as *Creation and Fall*)

1933

January 30	Adolf Hitler named Reich Chancellor of Germany
February 1	Bonhoeffer gives radio talk, "The Führer and the Individual in the Younger Generation"
April 7	Law for the Restoration of the Civil Service (includes the so-called Aryan paragraph)
April	Bonhoeffer writes essay "The Church and the Jewish Question" (published in June)

Summer semester	Bonhoeffer gives Christology lectures
August	Bonhoeffer involved in work on the Bethel Confession
September 5–6	Church Aryan paragraph implemented in the Old Prussian Union churches
September 11	Founding of the Pastors Emergency League with Martin Niemöller and others
September 27	Bonhoeffer and others protest at national synod in Wittenberg
October 17	Bonhoeffer begins service as an overseas pastor to two German congregations in London
November 13	German Christian Sports Palace rally in Berlin

1934

February 8–9	German Church Foreign Office delegation led by Theodor Heckel visits churches in London
May 31	Barmen Theological Declaration passed by the Confessing Synod of the German Evangelical Church in Wuppertal-Barmen
August 18–30	Participation in the conferences of the World Alliance and the Ecumenical Council in Fanø, Denmark; Bonhoeffer gives talk on "The Church and the Peoples of the World"

1935

Spring	Bonhoeffer visits Christian monastic communities in England
April 15	Bonhoeffer returns to Germany
April 26	Bonhoeffer takes up duties as director of a Confessing Church preachers' seminary, first in Zingsthof, then as of June in Finkenwalde. Eberhard Bethge attends first session. Bonhoeffer delivers lectures on "discipleship" in all five sessions (book is published in 1937). Bonhoeffer meets Ruth von Kleist-Retzow and her granddaughter Maria von Wedemeyer

Fall	Establishment of a House of Brethren to oversee the work at Finkenwalde
Winter semester	Bonhoeffer lectures in Berlin on "discipleship"
December 2	Enactment of the Fifth Implementation Decree of the Law to Restore Order in the German Evangelical Church as well as bans on Confessing Church examinations and ordination

1936

February 29–March 10	Bonhoeffer travels with his seminarians to Denmark and Sweden
June	Bonhoeffer writes essay "On the Question of Church Communion"
August 5	Bonhoeffer's permission to teach at the university is withdrawn
August 21–25	Bonhoeffer participates in the conference of the Ecumenical Council in Chamby

1937

July 1	Arrest and imprisonment of Martin Niemöller
August 29	Confessing Church preachers' seminaries are banned
September 28	Gestapo closes the preachers' seminary in Finkenwalde
December 5	Bonhoeffer continues to train seminarians illegally through the collective underground pastorates in Pomerania

1938

January 11	Gestapo ban on Bonhoeffer traveling to Berlin
April 20	All pastors ordered to swear loyalty oath to Hitler
September 9	Gerhard and Sabine Leibholz emigrate to London

September/ October	Bonhoeffer works on *Life Together*, the book about the experiences in Finkenwalde (published in 1939)
November 9	"Kristallnacht" pogroms throughout Germany and Austria

1939

March/April	Bonhoeffer travels to London, visiting his sister Sabine and meeting with Bishop Bell, Willem Visser 't Hooft, and Reinhold Niebuhr
June 2	Departure with his brother Karl-Friedrich to New York via London
June 12	Arrival in New York
June 20	Bonhoeffer decides to return to Germany
July 7/8	Bonhoeffer leaves New York together with his brother, returning to Germany via London
July 26	Arrival in Germany
September 1	Invasion of Poland and beginning of the Second World War
End of October	Beginning of the final underground pastorate in Sigurdshof

1940

Publication of *The Prayerbook of the Bible: An Introduction to the Psalms*

March 18	Gestapo closes the underground pastorates
August 22	Bonhoeffer banned from public speaking throughout the Reich
Probably end of October	Bonhoeffer receives assignment as secret agent for the Office of Military Intelligence through his brother-in-law Hans von Dohnanyi; assigned to Munich office. Begins work on his *Ethics* (published by Eberhard Bethge in 1949), particularly between November 1940–February 1941 in the Benedictine monastery of Ettal

1941

March 19	Bonhoeffer prohibited from publishing
February 24–March 24	Bonhoeffer travels to Switzerland on behalf of Military Intelligence
August 29–September 26	Bonhoeffer travels to Switzerland on behalf of Military Intelligence

1942

April 10–18	Bonhoeffer travels to Norway with Helmuth James von Moltke
May 11–26	Bonhoeffer makes his third and final trip to Switzerland
May 30–June 2	Bonhoeffer travels to Sweden; meets with Bishop Bell
June 8	Bonhoeffer re-encounters Maria von Wedemeyer
June 26–July 10	Bonhoeffer travels with Hans von Dohnanyi to Italy; conversations with officials in the Vatican

1943

January 13	Engagement to Maria von Wedemeyer
April 5	Bonhoeffer arrested, together with Hans and Christine von Dohnanyi; Bonhoeffer taken to Tegel military prison; interrogated by Manfred Roeder. In the two years that follow Bonhoeffer writes prison letters to his family and Eberhard Bethge (*Letters and Papers from Prison*, first published in Germany in 1951), as well as the letters to Maria von Wedemeyer (*Love Letters from Cell 92*, published in English in 1995)

1944

July 20	Failed attempt on Hitler's life by Claus Schenk Graf von Stauffenberg
September 22	Discovery of Dohnanyi's secret archive in Zossen

October 1	Arrests of Klaus Bonhoeffer and Rüdiger Schleicher
October 8	Dietrich Bonhoeffer moved to the underground prison at the Reich Central Security Headquarters prison

1945

February 7	Bonhoeffer moved with other prisoners to Buchenwald concentration camp
April 3	Bonhoeffer transported from Buchenwald
April 6	Prison transport stops in Schönberg, Bavaria
April 8	Bonhoeffer taken to Flossenbürg concentration camp and sentenced to death
April 9	Bonhoeffer hanged to death in Flossenbürg together with Hans Oster and Wilhelm Canaris

BIBLIOGRAPHY

Texts by Dietrich Bonhoeffer

Bismarck, Ruth-Alice, and Ulrich Kabitz, eds. *Brautbriefe Zelle 92: Dietrich Bonhoeffer-Maria von Wedemeyer, 1943–1945.* Munich: C. H. Beck'sche Verlagsbuchhandlung, 1992. Eng. trans.: *Love Letters from Cell 92: The Correspondence between Dietrich Bonhoeffer and Maria von Wedemeyer 1943–45.* Trans. John Brownjohn, with a postscript by Eberhard Bethge. London: HarperCollins, 1994/Nashville: Abingdon, 1995.

Bonhoeffer, Dietrich. *Dietrich Bonhoeffer Werke.* 17 vols. Ed. Eberhard Bethge, et al. Munich: Chr. Kaiser Verlag/Gütersloh: Gütersloher Verlagshaus, 1986–99. Eng. trans.: *Dietrich Bonhoeffer Works* (DBWE). Victoria J. Barnett, Wayne Whitson Floyd Jr., and Barbara Wojhoski, general editors. 17 vols. Minneapolis: Fortress Press, 1996–2014:

DBWE 1   *Sanctorum Communio.* 1998. Ed. Clifford J. Green. Trans. Reinhard Krauss and Nancy Lukens.

DBWE 2   *Act and Being.* Ed. Wayne Whitson Floyd, Jr. Trans. H. Martin Rumscheidt

DBWE 3   *Creation and Fall.* 1997. Ed. John W. De Gruchy. Trans. Douglas Stephen Bax.

DBWE 4   *Discipleship.* 2001. Ed. John D. Godsey and Geffrey B. Kelly. Trans. Barbara Green and Reinhard Krauss.

DBWE 5   *Life Together and Prayerbook of the Bible.* 1996. Ed. Geffrey B. Kelly. Trans. Daniel W. Bloesch and James H. Burtness.

DBWE 6   *Ethics.* 2005. Ed. Clifford J. Green. Trans. Reinhard Krauss, Douglas W. Stott, and Charles C. West.

DBWE 7   *Fiction from Tegel Prison.* Ed. Clifford J. Green. Trans. Nancy Lukens

DBWE 8   *Letters and Papers from Prison.* 2010. Ed. John W. De Gruchy. Trans. Isabel Best, Lisa E. Dahill, Reinhard Krauss, and Nancy Lukens.

DBWE 9   *The Young Bonhoeffer: 1918–1927.* 2003. Ed. Clifford J. Green, Marshall D. Johnson, and Paul Duane Matheny. Trans. Mary C. Nebelsick and Douglas W. Stott.

DBWE 10   *Barcelona, Berlin, New York: 1928–1931.* 2008. Ed. Clifford J. Green. Trans. Douglas W. Stott.

DBWE 11   *Ecumenical, Academic, and Pastoral Work: 1931–1932.* 2012. Ed. Victoria J. Barnett, Mark Brocker, and Michael B. Lukens. Trans. Isabel Best, Nicholas S. Humphrey, Marion Pauck, Anne Schmidt-Lange, and Douglas W. Stott.

DBWE 12   *Berlin: 1932–1933.* 2009. Ed. Larry L. Rasmussen. Trans. Isabel Best, David Higgins, and Douglas W. Stott.

DBWE 13   *London, 1933–1935.* 2007. Ed. Keith Clements. Trans. Isabel Best.

DBWE 14   *Theological Education at Finkenwalde: 1935–1937.* 2013. Ed. H. Gaylon Barker and Mark Brocker. Trans. Douglas W. Stott.

DBWE 15   *Theological Education Underground: 1937–1940.* 2012. Ed. Victoria J. Barnett. Trans. Victoria J. Barnett, Claudia D. Bergmann, Peter Frick, and Scott A. Moore.

DBWE 16   *Conspiracy and Imprisonment, 1940–1945.* 2006. Ed. Mark Brocker. Trans. Lisa E. Dahill.

Gremmels, Christian, and Wolfgang Huber, eds. *Dietrich Bonhoeffer Auswahl.* 6 vols. Gütersloh: Gütersloher Verlagshaus, 2006.

Secondary Literature

Barth, Friederike. *Die Wirklichkeit des Guten: Dietrich Bonhoeffers Ethik und ihr philosophischer Hintergrund.* Tübingen: Mohr Siebeck, 2011.

Barth, Karl. *Die Menschlichkeit Gottes.* Zollikon-Zurich: Theologischer Verlag, 1956.

————. *Römerbrief.* 2d ed. Zurich: Theologischer Verlag, 1922.

Besier, Gerhard. *Die Kirchen und das Dritte Reich: Spaltungen und Abwehrkämpfe 1934–1937.* Berlin: Propyläen, 2001.

Bethge, Eberhard. *Dietrich Bonhoeffer: Theologe—Christ—Zeitgenosse; Eine Biographie.* 1967. Ninth ed. Munich: Chr. Kaiser Verlag, 2005. Eng. trans.: *Dietrich Bonhoeffer: A Biography,* under the editorship of Edwin Robertson. Trans. Eric Mosbacher, Peter Ross, Betty Ross, Frank Clarke, and William Glen-Doepel. Rev. and ed. Victoria J. Barnett, based on the seventh German edition. Minneapolis: Fortress Press, 2000.

Burgsmüller, Alfred, and Rudolf Weth, eds. *Die Barmer Theologische Erklärung. Einführung und Dokumentation.* 6th ed. Neukirchen-Vluyn: Neukirchener Verlag, 1998.

Dietrich Bonhoeffer Jahrbuch/Yearbook. Vols. 1–5. Gütersloh: Gütersloher Verlagshaus, 2003–2012.

Dramm, Sabine. *Dietrich Bonhoeffer: Eine Einführung in sein Denken.* Gütersloh: Gütersloher Verlagshaus, 2001. Eng. trans.: *Dietrich Bonhoeffer: An Introduction to His Thought.* Trans. Thomas Rice. Peabody, MA: Hendrickson, 2007.

————. *V-Mann Gottes und der Abwehr? Dietrich Bonhoeffer und der Widerstand.* Gütersloh: Gütersloher Verlagshaus, 2005. Eng. trans.: *Dietrich Bonhoeffer and the Resistance.* Trans. Margaret Kohl. Minneapolis: Fortress Press, 2009.

Feil, Ernst. *Die Theologie Dietrich Bonhoeffers. Hermeneutik—Christologie—Weltverständnis.* Gesellschaft und Theologie, Abteilung Systematische Beiträge 6. Fifth ed. Munich and Mainz: Chr. Kaiser Verlag, 1996. Eng. trans.: *The Theology of Dietrich Bonhoeffer.* Trans. Martin Rumscheidt. Philadelphia: Fortress Press, 1985.

Haynes, Stephen R. *The Bonhoeffer Phenomenon: Portraits of a Protestant Saint.* Minneapolis: Fortress Press, 2004.

Henkys, Jürgen. *Geheimnis der Freiheit: Die Gedichte Dietrich Bonhoeffers aus der Haft. Biographie, Poesie, Theologie.* Gütersloh: Gütersloher Verlagshaus, 2005.

Hockenos, Matthew. *A Church Divided: German Protestants Confront the Nazi Past.* Bloomington: Indiana University Press, 2004.

International Bonhoeffer Forum. Vols. 1–10. Munich: Chr. Kaiser Verlag, 1976–1996.

International Bonhoeffer Interpretations. Series. Frankfurt: Lang Publishers, 2008–.

Jüngel, Eberhard. *Wertlose Wahrheit: zur Identität und Relevanz des christlichen Glaubens.* Munich: Chr. Kaiser Verlag, 1990.

Leibholz, Sabine. "Kindheit und Elternhaus." In Wolf-Dieter Zimmermann, ed., *Begegnungen mit Dietrich Bonhoeffer. Ein Almanach,* 12–27. 2d ed. Munich: Chr. Kaiser Verlag, 1965.

Leibholz-Bonhoeffer, Sabine. *Vergangen, erlebt, überwunden. Schicksale der Familie Bonhoeffer.* Gütersloh: Gütersloher Verlagshaus, 1968; 8th ed. 1995. New English ed.: *The Bonhoeffers: Portrait of a Family,* Chicago: Covenant Publications, 1994.

Die Mündige Welt. Vols. 1–5. Munich: Chr. Kaiser Verlag, 1955–1969. Eng. trans. (selected essays): Ronald Gregor Smith, ed., *World Come of Age.* Philadelphia: Fortress Press, 1967.

Oberman, Heiko A., et al., eds. *Kirchen- und Theologiegeschichte in Quellen*, vol. IV/2. Neukirchen-Vluyn: Neukirchener Verlag, 1980.

Schlingensiepen, Ferdinand. *Dietrich Bonhoeffer 1906–1945: Eine Biographie.* Munich: Beck, 2005. Eng. trans.: *Dietrich Bonhoeffer 1906–1945: Martyr, Thinker, Man of Resistance.* Trans. Isabel Best. London: Bloomsbury T&T Clark, 2012.

Schmitz, Florian. *"Nachfolge": Zur Theologie Dietrich Bonhoeffers.* Göttingen: Vandenhoeck & Ruprecht, 2013.

Scholder, Klaus. *Die Kirchen und das Dritte Reich.* Vol. I: *Vorgeschichte und Zeit der Illusionen 1918–1934.* Frankfurt am Main: Ullstein, 1977. Eng. trans. *Preliminary History and the Time of Illusions 1918–1934.* Trans. John Bowden. Philadelphia: Fortress Press, 1988. Vol II: *Das Jahr der Ernüchterung 1934: Barmen und Rom.* 2d ed. Berlin: W. J. Siedler, 1988 (c. 1985). Eng. trans.: *The Churches and the Third Reich*, vol. 2: *The Year of Disillusionment 1934—Barmen and Rome.* Trans. John Bowden. London/Minneapolis: SCM Press/Fortress Press, 1988.

Smid, Marikje. *Deutscher Protestantismus und Judentum, 1932/1933.* Munich: Chr. Kaiser Verlag, 1990.

Strohm, Christoph. *Die Kirchen im Dritten Reich.* Munich: Beck, 2011.

———. *Theologische Ethik im Kampf gegen den Nationalsozialismus. Der Weg Dietrich Bonhoeffers mit den Juristen Hans von Dohnanyi und Gerhard Leibholz in den Widerstand.* Munich: Chr. Kaiser Verlag, 1989.

Tietz, Christiane. "Dietrich Bonhoeffer (1906–1945): Theologe im Widerstand." In Jürgen Kampmann, ed., *Protestantismus in Preußen. Vom Ersten Weltkrieg bis zur deutschen Teilung*, 291–312. Frankfurt am Main: Hansisches Dr.- und Verl.-Haus, 2011.

———, ed., *Bonhoeffer Handbuch.* Forthcoming. Tübingen: Mohr Siebeck.

Tödt, Ilse, ed. *Die Finkenwalder Rundbriefe. Briefe und Texte von Dietrich Bonhoeffer und seinen Predigerseminaristen 1935–1946.* Gütersloh: Gütersloher Verlagshaus, 2013.

INDEX